GREYSTONE'S
Creative Hands

EDITOR

Beverley Hilton

GREYSTONE PRESS/NEW YORK · TORONTO · LONDON

Volume 12

Contents

Shaping up to belts

This chapter gives the basic method for making three types of belts — straight, shaped (there are graph patterns for two shapes) and crushed. With this know-how you can go on and make a whole collection of beautiful belts in different fabrics with a variety of fastenings. Junk stores are treasure troves for buckles and clasps.

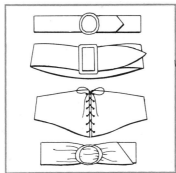

Materials for stiff belts

Top fabrics
Belts can be made from many materials. Any gay dress or home furnishing fabric will make an attractive belt. Leather, braids, velvet and suede are especially suitable as they are hard wearing, look attractive and provide a contrast to any garment.

Natural linen is a practical choice to tone in with all outfits. And for a really exclusive effect try making a belt from tapestry type fabric.

Stiffenings
☐ Back-a-belt kits
☐ Belting
☐ Non-woven interfacings such as heavy weight Pellon
☐ Tailor's canvas (this must be washed first as it shrinks in washing)
☐ Buckram
☐ Valance canvas which is obtainable in upholstery departments

Backings
Good quality taffeta, strong silk, skiver (thinly sliced leather) and soft leather are the most suitable. Felt is also used sometimes, but remember that it isn't washable.

Miscellaneous
☐ UHU glue for sticking belts
☐ Punch and eyelets
☐ Buckles for self-covering or decorative fastenings such as contrasting buckles, clasps, belt hooks and lacing

Straight belt

What you will need
Top fabric or braid, interfacing in the form of a back-a-belt kit, buckram or other interfacing. Your own choice of fastening.

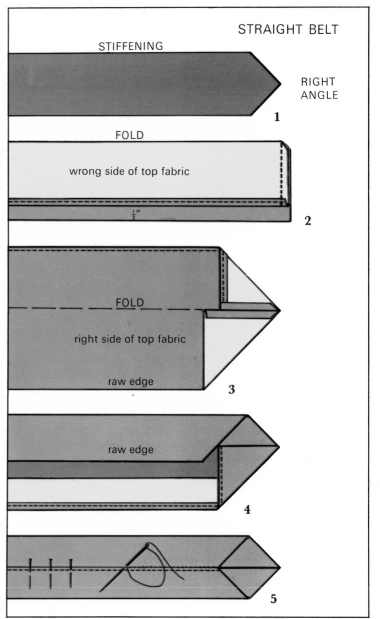

▲ **1.** *Cut stiffening into point* **2.** *Stitch one end of top fabric* **3.** *Fold seam into point* **4.** *Fold raw edge over stiffening* **5.** *Finishing back of belt*

Making the belt
Decide on the width you want the belt and cut the stiffening to the exact width, and to the length of your waist measurement plus 6 inches.

Cut one end of the stiffening into a right-angled point (figure **1**).

Cut a strip of top fabric twice the belt width plus $\frac{3}{4}$ inch and $\frac{3}{4}$ inch longer than the stiffening.

Turn in one long edge of the top fabric for $\frac{1}{4}$ inch and stitch.

Fold the top fabric lengthwise with the stitched edge $\frac{1}{2}$ inch in from the raw edge and right sides together (figure **2**). Pin and stitch the end securely with a $\frac{1}{4}$ inch seam as shown.

Trim the corner of the seam allowance and then, following figure **3**, fold into a point with the seam falling on the first fold and press the seam open.

Turn to the right side. Place the belt stiffening into the point and fold the raw edge over as shown (figure **4**). Press.

Fold and press the finished edge over the raw edge (figure **5**).

Pin the edge into position and hand-sew with very small hemming stitches.

Attach a buckle or clasp of your choice to finish.

1211

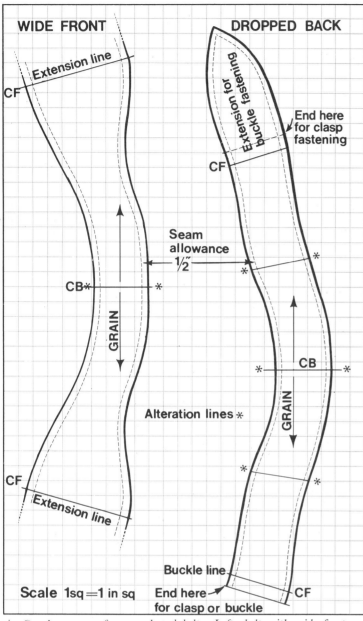

WIDE FRONT   DROPPED BACK

Extension line

CF

Extension for buckle fastening

End here for clasp fastening

CF

Seam allowance ½"

CB*   *

GRAIN

CB

GRAIN

Alteration lines *

CF

Extension line

Buckle line

Scale 1sq =1 in sq   End here for clasp or buckle   CF

▲ *Graph patterns for two shaped belts. Left: belt with wide front and narrow back. Right: belt of uniform width with lower back*

Shaped belt

Two patterns are given for shaped belts. One of these is for a belt which is wide at the front and narrower at the back. The other is a uniform width but slopes down at the back.

The patterns
Choose the belt shape from the patterns and draw the belt pattern on 1 inch squared graph paper. The patterns are for a 26 inch waist, so alter them to your measurement where indicated. The patterns include ½ inch seam allowance.

What you will need
Top fabric and interfacing (self-adhesive or otherwise) or tailor's canvas.
Felt, lining fabric or self fabric for the backing and your choice of fastening.
If you are using a felt backing you will need UHU glue.

A bunch of beautiful belts, laced, buckled and braid trimmed ▶

Making the belt

Cut out the top fabric and the interfacing the exact size of the pattern, placing the pattern straight of grain line on the lengthwise grain of the fabric.

Attach the interfacing to the wrong side of the fabric. Do this with a row of stitches within the seam allowance, or stick them together if a self-adhesive interfacing is being used. The two fabrics are now used as one.

Snip the long curved edges at $\frac{1}{4}$ inch intervals up to the seamline, which is $\frac{1}{2}$ inch from the edge (figure **6**). Press the edges to the wrong side as shown (figure **7**).

Felt backing. If you are using a felt backing cut the felt $\frac{1}{16}$ inch narrower than the desired belt width and stick to the inside.

Attach a buckle or clasp to finish.

Fabric backing. If you are using lining or self fabric backing use the pattern to cut two layers of the fabric. Stitch the two layers together with right sides facing just inside the seamline, leaving an opening for turning.

Turn to the right side and close the opening.

Pin the backing to the wrong side of the belt and topstitch in place or sew firmly with a very small hemming stitch.

Crushed belt

The fabric for this belt is cut straight and the belt is most effectively made in soft leather, velvet or satin materials.

What you will need

A fairly soft interfacing such as Pellon. Top fabric as above, and lining fabric for the backing.

Making the belt

Cut out the top fabric and interfacing 1 inch wider than the desired width of the belt and to your waist measurement plus 6 inches. Also cut the lining fabric to the same length but $\frac{1}{16}$ inch narrower. This is so that the lining will roll in nicely at the edges and not show on the outside.

Shape one end of all the layers as shown (figure **8**).

Baste the interfacing to the wrong side of the top fabric and use as one.

Place the lining and the top fabric together, right sides facing, and stitch all around taking $\frac{1}{2}$ inch seam allowance and leaving the straight end unstitched. The shaped end of the belt will have to be eased slightly onto the lining fabric, which was cut slightly narrower. Trim the seam allowance of the interfacing close to the stitches as shown (figure **9**). Then trim the other seams and the corners.

Turn to the right side.

Attach a buckle narrower than the belt to give a crushed effect as shown (figure **10**).

Paper ring fastening

The paper ring fastening used (figure **11**) has a 2 inch diameter. Make a straight belt as shown in the previous instructions, but make it only 4 inches longer than your waist measurement and narrow enough to fit through the ring.

Make both ends pointed.

Complete the fastening by turning each point back and stitching them securely in place (figure **12**).

6. *Shaped belt: snip seam allowance every $\frac{1}{4}$ in* **7.** *Press snipped edges to inside* **8.** *Crushed belt: shape one end* **9.** *Trim seam allowances and corners* **10.** *Attach buckle* **11.** *Paper ring fastening* **12.** *Ring attached* ▶

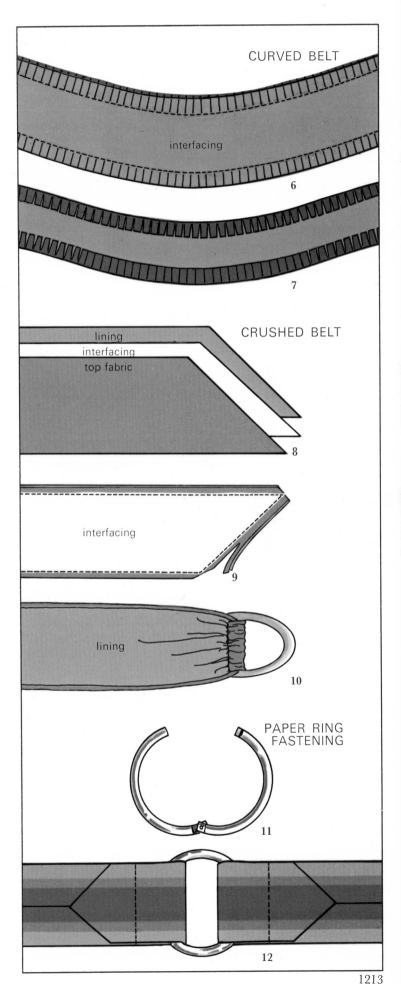

CURVED BELT

interfacing

6

7

CRUSHED BELT

lining
interfacing
top fabric

8

interfacing

9

lining

10

PAPER RING FASTENING

11

12

Linen bread basket to sew

You can make this simple but effective bread basket in an evening. It is made from three fabric hexagons and a tracing pattern is given opposite for a sixth of each hexagon. With six pockets for bread rolls and a central space for bread sticks, the bread basket is a practical addition to any table. The large outer hexagon acts as a base and catches the inevitable crumbs. Easily laundered, the bread basket can be used over and over again, and stored flat.

You will need

For the bread basket:
- ☐ ½yd 36in wide green linen
- ☐ ½yd 36in wide white linen
- ☐ 2½yds ½in wide flat white braid
- ☐ 2¾yds narrow white cotton lace
- ☐ Pins
- ☐ Fabric cutting scissors
- ☐ Matching sewing threads, basting thread
- ☐ Embroidery floss, embroidery needle

For pattern making:
- ☐ Large sheet of brown paper
- ☐ Pencil and tracing paper
- ☐ Piece of stiff cardboard at least 9 inches square
- ☐ Scissors

Making the patterns

Using the tracing paper, trace the triangle and mark line X to Y. Transfer the shape to the cardboard and cut out accurately. Place the cardboard template on the brown paper and draw carefully around the edge. Repeat this five more times, building up a hexagon as shown in figure **1**. Build up

another hexagon on the brown paper in the same way. Cut out both hexagons.

Cut the cardboard template along the line X to Y and build up a smaller hexagon on the brown paper as before. Cut this out. You will now have 2 hexagons with 8¼ inch sides and 1 hexagon with 7 inch sides.

Cutting the fabric

Pin the 7 inch and one of the 8¼ inch paper hexagons to the green linen and cut around the edge of each pattern without seam allowance.

Pin the other 8¼ inch paper hexagon to the white linen and cut around the edge of the pattern (no seam allowance).

Applying the lace and braid

Make narrow ¼ inch turned hems around the edges of the two large hexagons.

Trim the hemmed edges with

the cotton lace, neatly sewing it on by hand.

Bind the raw edges of the small green linen hexagon with flat braid by folding the braid over the edges and hemming it into place. (You may find this easier to do if you starch the small green linen hexagon first.)

Cut the remaining braid into six 8 inch lengths. Fold each length in half lengthwise, stitch the edges together and turn in the ends.

Sew a length of braid to the center of each side of the small green linen hexagon (figure 2). Tie a knot at the end of each length of braid.

Decorate the large green hexagon with tiny flowers embroidered into each corner.

Assembling the bread basket

Baste and then sew the small green linen hexagon to the white linen hexagon as shown in figure 3, using either lines of neat backstitches or machine stitches.

Backstitch or machine stitch the white hexagon to the large green hexagon as shown in figure 4. Make sure that the ends of the seams are finished off firmly and neatly.

Tie the six lengths of braid together and you will see that this pulls the hexagons into the shape shown in the picture.

Finishing

Before you use the bread basket it is necessary to starch it for a crisp, fresh finish.

Undo the ties and the hexagons will lie flat. Wash the bread basket and starch it with a fairly strong solution of starch. Iron while it is still damp with a hot iron.

You may find that you need to separate the layers as the starch sometimes causes them to stick together.

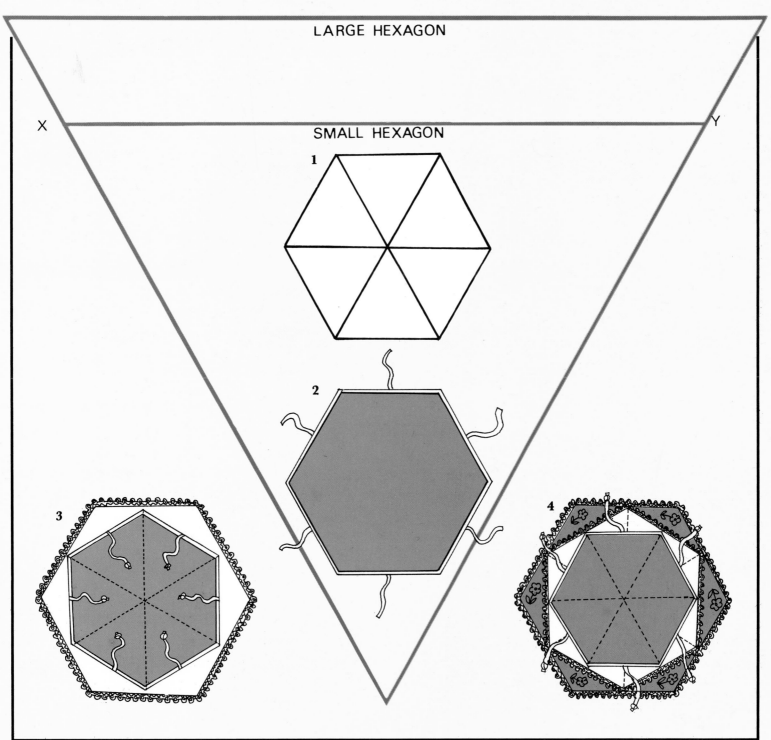

LARGE HEXAGON

SMALL HEXAGON

X   Y

1

2

3

4

1215

Straight skirts and all about pleats

Dress-making 61

There is always a place in every woman's wardrobe for a straight skirt, so this chapter starts with a very simple adaptation of the Creative Hands basic skirt pattern in Dressmaking chapter 4, page 76, to this style.

The elegance of a straight fitted skirt must be considered in relation to the more practical aspect of movement; sometimes this style can be a little restricting to wear because there is only as much fullness around the hem as the hip measurement will allow. This chapter covers pleats which can be used in conjunction with a straight skirt to give more width at the hem or which can be used with other skirt styles to become an integral part of the design. Pleats for shaped seams and box pleating are also included, and once you've absorbed the basic instructions, you can enjoy playing with pleats to create design ideas of your own.

▼ *Details of the straight skirt*

▼ **1.** *The straight skirt pattern*

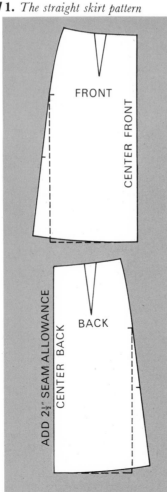

FRONT

CENTER FRONT

BACK

CENTER BACK

ADD 2½" SEAM ALLOWANCE

From left to right:
1. single inverted pleat in the Center Back seam of the straight skirt; **2.** the double pleat in a straight Center Back seam; **3.** fan pleats in the straight panel seam version of the six-gore skirt; **4.** the inverted pleat in the six-gore skirt with flared panel seams; **5.** straight box pleats falling from the hipline; **6.** shaped box pleats for a full length evening skirt.

1

The straight skirt

Suitable fabrics
Choose a firmly woven fabric because there is a great deal more strain on the seams than in a full skirt.

Reshaping the pattern
Take the basic skirt pattern from Dressmaking chapter 4 and straighten the side seams from the hipline, and also straighten the hem as shown (figure **1**).
Cut out the pattern along the new lines.

Layout and cutting notes,
Make an extra deep seam allowance of 2½ inches along the Center

2   3   4   5   6

Back seam for extra strength over the seat of the skirt. You can use the deep seam allowance to insert a Dior pleat as shown further on.

Inserting the zipper
For a smooth finish over the side hip, stitch the zipper into the Center Back seam rather than at the side. Use the method for a zipper in a straight seam shown in Dressmaking 8, page 156.
The rest of the skirt is made like the basic flared skirt, Dressmaking chapter 4 to 7, pages 76, 96, 116 and 136.

About pleats

The Dior pleat is an ideal choice if you want to give more width at the hem of a straight fitted skirt. This pleat will keep the smooth line of the skirt, and it always remains flat because it is just a piece of fabric set across the seam allowance of the Center Back seam. The Dior pleat was specially designed to give the flattest finish regardless of fabric.
But, provided the fabric is crisp, other types of seam pleats can look very attractive, and if made carefully they do not necessarily create bulk.
The inverted pleat works well in panel seams such as in the panels of the six-gore skirt or the four-gore skirt (see Dressmaking chapters 27, page 536 and 14, page 276, for the pattern variations).
Following the inverted pleat are double and fan pleats which must be made with even greater care since the pleats use more fabric and the weight could distort the hang of the garment.
Also included here are box pleats, both straight and shaped.

The Dior pleat

Preparing the Center Back seam for the pleat

Cut the Center Back seam with $2\frac{1}{2}$ inch seam allowance, stitch to within $5\frac{1}{2}$ inches of the hemline, and fasten off the stitches securely. Leave the rest of the seam basted together as far as the hemline. Make the skirt hem in the usual way, but this time take the hem through the seam allowance at the Center Back as shown (figure **2**). Then turn back the seam allowance and hand sew to the hem using a felling stitch on the seam edges and an invisible slip stitch along the edge of the hem (figure **3**). Press flat, leaving the seam basted.

Preparing the pleat backing

Cut a piece of fabric about 8 inches long and 6 inches wide from the skirt remnants. Turn under 2 inches along one 6 inch edge and make a hem. Turn back the remaining edges $\frac{1}{2}$ inch all around and hem to the wrong side with small catch stitches (figure **4**).

Finishing the pleat

Place the Center Back seam of the skirt, wrong side up, over an ironing board and lay the pleat backing over the basted seam with the hemmed edge $\frac{1}{2}$ inch up from the skirt hemline. Make sure that the pleat backing is absolutely square, otherwise it will tilt when you wear the skirt. Baste and stitch to the seam allowance as shown (figure **5**) catching the seam allowance only and not the outside of the skirt as well.

Remove all basting before pressing.

Single inverted pleat—straight seam

The single inverted pleat is often used in the Center Back seam of a skirt, when it is called a kick pleat. The depth of the pleat may be dictated by the width of your fabric, but if you are an average size you should be able to measure out for a pleat which is 2 inches to the pleat fold on each side. For pleat fold see Dressmaking 13, page 256.

Cutting out

Fold the fabric and lay out the Back pattern piece as follows.

Following figure **6**, measure out 4 inches from the fold to the length of the pattern and baste the fabric together along this line. This will become the Center Back line. Also make a row of basting stitches along the fold itself.

Place the skirt Back pattern to the first
1218

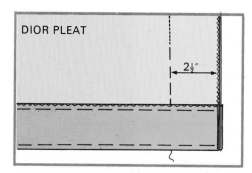

▲ **2.** *Taking the hem through the seam allowance*

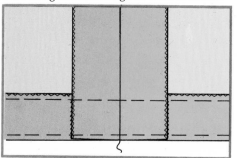

▲ **3.** *The seam allowance hand-sewn at the hem*

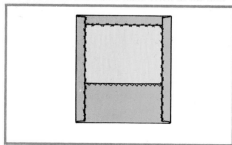

▲ **4.** *The completed pleat backing*

basted line as shown. Cut out the pattern to include the extension for the pleat and mark all other pattern details.

Making the pleat

Open out the Back on an ironing board and bring the basted Center Back line to meet the basted fold line (figure **7**). Pin lightly and press, avoiding the pins.

Fit the skirt.

After fitting, work as follows. Measure from the hemline up the length you want the pleat (figure **8**) and from the waist measure out the Center Back zipper opening. Stitch the rest of the Center Back seam as shown.

Baste the pleat in position and cut off the surplus pleat backing from the waist edge to $1\frac{1}{2}$ inches above the top of the pleat (figure **9**).

Hand sew the loose edge of the pleat backing to the deep seam allowance across the top of the pleat.

On the outside, hand work a bar at the top of the pleat, catching the fabric of the pleat backing to strengthen this point.

When making the hem be sure that the pleat hem is slightly shorter than the outside hem.

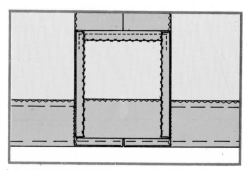

▲ **5.** *The pleat backing stitched in place*

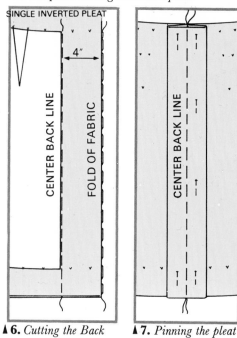

▲ **6.** *Cutting the Back*   ▲ **7.** *Pinning the pleat*

The double pleat

Another attractive type of pleat to make in a straight seam is the double pleat. This is two pleats, one over the other.

If this pleat is used in the Center Back seam of the skirt it must be kept quite short as the weight of the fabric could make it look very untidy.

Cutting out

This pleat is not cut onto the width of the skirt. Usually there is not enough fabric to spare at the sides of a layout to include a pleat of this width, so the fabric for pleating is cut separately.

Cut the Center Back seam with a $2\frac{1}{2}$ inch seam allowance. This gives you the half pleat depth plus $\frac{1}{2}$ inch seam allowance.

Making the pleat

Baste the Center Back seam and press open. After fitting the skirt, stitch the Center Back seam to within 6 inches of the hemline, leaving an opening at the top for the zipper.

To make the pleat backing for the double inverted pleat, cut a piece of fabric $9\frac{1}{2}$ inches long and 13 inches wide and make

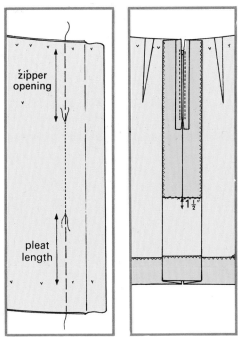

▲ 8. *Stitching the seam* **▲ 9.** *The finished pleat*

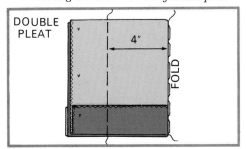

▲ 10. *Preparing the backing for the pleat*

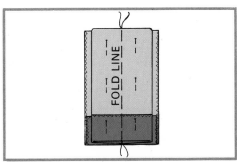

▲ 11. *The basted and pressed backing*

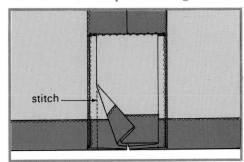

▲ 12. *The backing stitched in place*

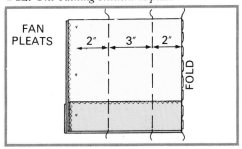

▲ 13. *Preparing the backing for the pleats*

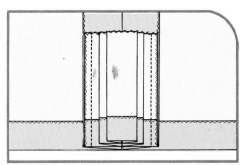

▲ 14. *The pleated backing stitched in place*

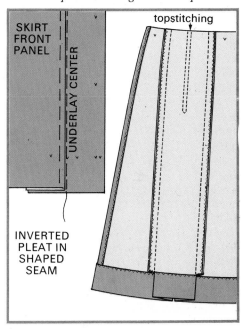

▲ 15. *Meeting the fold edges on the underlay*

a hem 2 inches deep along one 13 inch edge.

Fold the fabric in half and baste together with a row of stitches 4 inches from the fold. Also trace baste the fold line (figure **10**). Now press the pleats into this piece as follows: With wrong side upward, bring the fold line to meet the basted line and pin. Press, making sure that you press the basted seam open (figure **11**).

Finish the hem on the skirt before attaching the pleat backing.

Pin and baste the prepared pleat backing to the deep seam allowance of the skirt Center Back seam and stitch in place, stitching the seam through the hem on both sides (figure **12**).

Stitch the top of the pleats to the seam allowance to secure.

Fan pleats for straight seam

Fan pleats are two or more pleats, one over the other, with the depth of the pleats lessening with each layer. In the example the pleat nearest the outside is 2 inches to the fold, the next 1½ inches and the third only one inch. This creates a pretty fan effect when the pleats spring open and looks particularly attractive made in a raw silk, which is light but firm. Fan pleats look very effective set into a straight paneled six-gore evening skirt with pleats starting just below knee level.

The pleats are made first on a separate piece of fabric (figure **13**), like the double pleat, and the pleated section is inserted in the same way (figure **14**).

Inverted pleats in shaped seams

Inverted pleats which go into shaped panel seams are made in two stages, as a straight pleat cut onto the width of the pattern would cause tightness on the inside of the pleat and the hem would twist. So on the panel seam it is best to cut up to the pleat fold only and back the pleat with another panel.

Cutting out

These instructions are given for the six-gore skirt (Dressmaking chapter 27), but the same technique applies to other curved seams.

When cutting out the six-gore skirt for inverted panel pleats, add 2½ inches seam allowance to each panel seam on the Front, side front, Back and side back pattern pieces.

For each pleat, cut an underlay 5 inches wide and the length of the skirt in the straight grain of the fabric, making four pieces in all.

Making the pleat

Mark the lengthwise center on each pleat underlay with basting stitches. Working on the skirt, fold under the seam allowance on each panel seam and bring the folded edges to meet on the center marking on the right side of the underlay (figure **15**). Baste in place and topstitch the pleats to the required length.

Press and stitch the underlay to the seam allowance of the panel seams.

There are two ways of finishing the hem. If the pleat depth does not twist, you can make a flat hem as for the child's pleated skirt (Dressmaking 13, p. 256). But if the hem is tight on the pleats, hem the skirt and the underlay separately and stitch through the hemline when stitching the panel in position (see figure **12**).

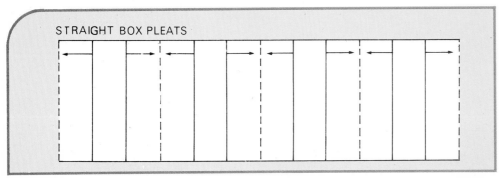

▲ 16. *Measuring out the fabric for pleating in a forward and reversing order*

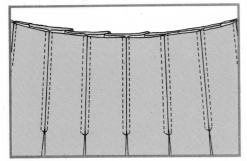

▲ 17. *The topstitched, waist fitted pleats*

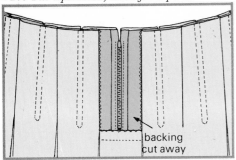

▲ 18. *Pleat backing cut away for the zipper*

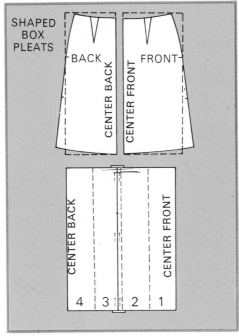

▲ 19. *Squaring off the basic skirt pattern*

Box pleating

Box pleating can be made in many ways, from the tiniest box pleated edging with pleats only $\frac{1}{2}$ inch apart to generous size box pleats on a skirt. In addition, the box pleats can be straight or shaped. Box pleating is a series of inverted pleats where double distance and double pleat depth alternate as you measure out the fabric for pleating. Each double distance must be carefully marked out so that all the pleats are of equal depth.

Straight box pleats

The same amount of fabric is required as for basic pleating (Dressmaking chapter 13, page 256).

Measure out the pleating as shown (figure **16**), then work the pleating from left to right in a forward and reversing order on the open length of fabric as shown by the arrows on the diagram.

If making a skirt, baste the pleats into the correct waist fitting by rolling each pleat edge under between hipline

1220

and waistline (see Dressmaking 31, p. 618). Press, then topstitch the pleats before joining the ends of the length (figure **17**). Insert the zipper into a pleat, cutting away the pleat backing far enough to allow the zipper fastener free movement (figure **18**).

Shaped box pleats

Here the width of each pleat tapers out toward the hem. Each pleat is cut in sections with individual underlays.

The pleats should therefore be spaced about 4 to 5 inches apart to avoid too much fabric inside the skirt and the pattern must be very carefully worked out.

Use the basic skirt pattern from Dressmaking 4, p. 76, and square it up through the hipline (figure **19**). Pin the pattern pieces together on the side seams as shown and divide into equal sections 4 to 5 inches apart, according to the amount you can accommodate on your hip size.

Pin the pattern with the Center Front $\frac{1}{2}$ inch from the straight edge of a sheet of paper. Cut the original pattern through the first pleat line and spread the pattern 1 inch apart. Continue to cut and spread

each section similarly, and mark each section after cutting so that you can match them up afterward (figure **20**).

On each cut section add $\frac{1}{2}$ inch at the hem edge and connect with a straight line to the hipline as shown so that each panel becomes flared.

Measure your waist measurement on the original pattern, divide the surplus on the new pattern by the number of pleats you are making, and taper each pleat into the waistline by this amount.

Cut out the new flared panel pattern pieces; when cutting out the fabric place the center of each panel on the straight of grain and cut out with $2\frac{1}{2}$ inch seams. The pleat underlay does not have to be the full length of each pleat, but only has to go $1\frac{1}{2}$ inches beyond the pleat stitching, and be hand-sewn to the pleat depth. Cut each underlay on the straight of grain to the required length, 5 inches wide. On each pleat underlay, turn up the hem then stitch to the panels (figure **21**).

Finalize the shaping at the waist edge at the fitting stage.

▼ 20. *The pattern sections cut and spread*

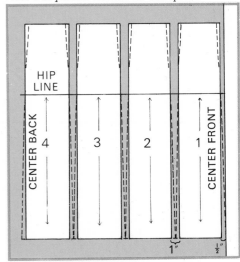

▼ 21. *The underlays stitched in place*

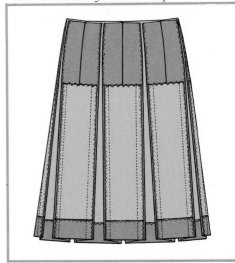

Pattern Library

Design inspiration

The sources of inspiration for embroidery design are endless. For instance, the design on a favorite tea or dinner service can be adapted for matching table linen. This enchanting design was adapted from a Josiah Wedgwood dinner service design named Columbia. The design would look pleasing centered on a tablecloth, and the dragons around the outer edge of the design could be adapted as a border for the cloth. The embroidery stitches used are mainly shaded long and short stitch with the scrolls and coils worked in satin stitch. Chain stitch and seeding have been used on the circular border enclosing the nosegay of flowers.

Seamless pullover in fisherman's knitting

Your first project in fisherman's knitting, a seamless sweater for an outdoor man. The firmness of the fabric, which results from the traditional stitch, makes this an ideal garment to wear in cold or windy weather.

Size

Directions are for 38in chest. The figures in brackets [] refer to the 40, 42 and 44in sizes respectively.
Length at center Back, 23[23: 23½:23½]in.
Sleeve seam, 18in, adjustable.

Gauge

7 sts and 9 rows to 1in over st st worked on No.3 circular needle.

Materials

Sports yarn
7[7:8:8] 2oz skeins
One No.2 14in or 24in circular needle
 (or Canadian No.11)
One No.3 14in or 24in circular needle
 (or Canadian No.10)
One set of 4 No.2 double-pointed needles
One set of 4 No.3 double-pointed needles

NB This pullover is entirely seamless and requires no finishing after knitting.
Yarn should be joined at side seams by leaving ends to darn into seam on completion.

Pullover

Using No.2 circular needle, cast on 264[276:288:300] sts.
1st row *P1, K2, P1, rep from * to end. Join into a
1222

circle and place marker thread before first st to mark beginning of round.
Next round *P1, K2, P1, rep from * to end of round. Rep last round until work measures 3in.
Change to No.3 circular needle.
Next round *P into front and back of next st to make one st, K130[136:142:148], P1, rep from * once.
Continue in st st with mock seam sts.
1st round *K1, P1, K130 [136:142:148], P1, rep from * once more.
2nd round *P2, K130[136: 142:148], P1, rep from * once more.
Rep 1st and 2nd rounds until work measures 12in from cast-on edge ending with a 1st round.
Begin yoke pattern and underarm gusset.
1st round *K into front and back and front of first st, P132[138:144:150], rep from * once more.
2nd round *K3, P132[138: 144:150], rep from * once more.
3rd round *K3, P1, K130 [136:142:148], P1, rep from * once more.
Rep 3rd round once more.
Rep 2nd round twice more.
7th round *Inc once in each of next 2 sts, K1, P1, K130 [136:142:148], P1, rep from * once more.
8th round *K5, P1, K130 [136:142:148], P1, rep from * once more.
9th round *K5, P132[138: 144:150], rep from * once more.
Rep 9th round once more.
Rep 8th round once more.

12th round *K5, P1, (K2, P2) 32[34:35:37] times, K2 [0:2:0], P1, rep from * once more.
13th round *Inc, K2, inc, K1, P1, K130[136:142:148], P1, rep from * once more.
14th round *K7, P1, (P2, K2) 32[34:35:37] times, P2 [0:2:0], P1, rep from * once more.
15th round *K7, P1, K130 [136:142:148], P1, rep from * once more.
Continue in this way, working center 130[136:142:148] sts in 4 row patt, keeping seam sts correct and inc one st at each side of each gusset on every 6th row until 14 rows more have been worked. There should now be 11 sts between seam sts on gusset.
Break yarn at end of last round.

Divide for armholes

Slip gusset sts and seam sts (13 sts at each side) onto holder or thread until needed. Work Front on center 130[136:142:148] sts working in rows.
**1st row P.
2nd row K.
3rd row K.
4th row P.
Rep 1st—4th rows once more then 1st and 2nd rows once.

Work center patt panel
1st patt row K.
2nd patt row P.
3rd patt row K2[5:8:11], *K10, P1, K10, rep from * to last 2[5:8:11] sts, K to end.
4th patt row K1, P1[4:7:10], * P9, K3, P9, rep from * to last 2[5:8:11] sts, P to last st, K1.
5th patt row K2[5:8:11], *K8, (P1, K1) twice, P1, K8, rep from * to last 2[5:8:11] sts, K to end.
6th patt row K1, P1[4:7:10], * P7, (K1, P2) 3 times, P5, rep from * to last 2[5:8:11] sts, P to last st, K1.
7th patt row K2[5:8:11], *K6, P1, K2, P3, K2, P1, K6, rep from * to last 2[5:8:11] sts, K to end.
8th patt row K1, P1[4:7:10], * P5, K1, P2, (K1, P1) 3 times, P1, K1, P5, rep from *

to last 2[5:8:11] sts, P to last st, K1.
9th patt row K2[5:8:11], *K4, (P1, K2) twice, P1, (K2, P1) twice, K4, rep from * to last 2[5:8:11] sts, K to end.
10th patt row K1, P1[4:7: 10], *P3, (K1, P2) twice, K3, (P2, K1) twice, P3, rep from * to last 2[5:8:11] sts, P to last st, K1.
11th patt row K2[5:8:11], *K5, P1, K2, (P1, K1) 3 times, K1, P1, K5, rep from * to last 2[5:8:11] sts, K to end.
12th patt row K1, P1[4:7: 10], *P4, (K1, P2) twice, (K1, P2) 3 times, P2, rep from * to last 2[5:8:11] sts, P to last st, K1.
13th patt row K2[5:8:11], *K6, P1, K2, P3, K2, P1, K6, rep from * to last 2[5:8:11] sts, K to end.
14th patt row K1, P1[4:7: 10], *P5,,K1, P2, (K1, P1) 3 times, P1, K1, P5, rep from * to last 2[5:8:11] sts, P to last st, K1.
15th patt row K2[5:8:11], *K7, (P1, K2) 3 times, K5, rep from * to last 2[5:8:11] sts, K to end.
16th patt row K1, P1[4:7: 10], *P6, K1, P2, K3, P2, K1, P6, rep from * to last 2[5:8: 11] sts, P to last st, K1.
17th patt row K2[5:8:11], *K8, (P1, K1) 3 times, K7, rep from * to last 2[5:8:11] sts, K to end.
18th patt row K1, P1[4:7: 10], *P7, (K1, P2) 3 times, P5, rep from * to last 2[5:8: 11] sts, P to last st, K1.
19th patt row K2[5:8:11], *K9, P3, K9, rep from * to last 2[5:8:11] sts, K to end.
20th patt row K1, P1[4:7: 10], *P8, (K1, P1) 3 times, P7, rep from * to last 2[5:8: 11] sts, P to last st, K1.
21st patt row K2[5:8:11], *K10, P1, K10, rep from * to last 2[5:8:11] sts, K to end.
22nd patt row K1, P1[4:7: 10], *P9, K3, P9, rep from * to last 2[5:8:11] sts, P to last st, K1.
23rd patt row As 21st.
24th patt row K1, P1[4:7: 10], *P10, K1, P10, rep from * to last 2[5:8:11] sts, P to last st, K1.

▲ *A modern interpretation of the traditional fisherman's pullover*

25th patt row K.
26th patt row P.
P 1 row. K 2 rows. P 1 row.
Rep last 4 rows once more.
P 1 row. K 2 rows.
Next row P2[0:2:0], *K2,
P2, rep from * to end.
K 1 row.

Next row K2[0:2:0], *P2,
K2, rep from * to end.
Rep last 4 rows until 14 rows
more have been worked.
P 1 row. K 1 row.

For 42 and 44in sizes only
K 1 row. P 2 rows. K 1 row.**

For all sizes divide for shoulders

1st row K48[50:52:54], then
complete this shoulder on
these sts.
***2nd row** P2 tog, P to end.
3rd row P to last 2 sts, P2
tog.
4th row K2 tog, K to end.
5th row K to last 2 sts, K2
tog.
6th row P2 tog, P to end.
7th row P to last 2 sts, P2
tog.
8th row K2 tog, K to end.
9th row K to last 2 sts, K2
tog.
P 2 rows. K 1 row.
Slip sts on holder.***
With RS facing, slip center
34[36:38:40] sts onto holder
and leave for neckband.
Attach yarn to rem sts and K
to end. Complete other
shoulder to correspond,
working from *** to ***,
reversing shaping.

Back

With RS facing, attach yarn
to rem 130[136:142:148] sts
and work from ** to ** as
for Front.

Work shoulders

K 1 row. P 2 rows. K 1 row.
Rep last 4 rows twice more.
Bind off right shoulder as
follows:
Hold Back and Front together
with WS touching.
Bind off both shoulders
together on RS by *K first
st from Back and Front tog,
K next 2 sts tog, lift first st
over 2nd, rep from * until all
shoulder stitches are bound off.
Slip center 50[52:54:56] sts
onto holder for neckband and
bind off 2nd shoulder in same
way.

Neckband

Using No.3 circular needle,
K sts from Back holder, pick up
and K 14 sts down right side of
neck, K across sts from Front
holder and pick up and K 14
sts up left side of neck.
1st round *P1, K2, P1, rep
from * to end.
Rep 1st round for 1in.
If preferred, neckband may be
made longer and folded in

half to WS and slip stitched in
place.

Sleeves

Using set of 4 No.3 dp needles,
with RS facing, work gusset
sts on first needle, P1, K11,
P1, pick up and K110[110:
118:118] sts evenly around
armhole, dividing the stitches
on 3 needles. Work in rounds.
1st round P1, K11, P1, K2,
*P2, K2, rep from * to end.
2nd round P1, K2 tog tbl,
K7, K2 tog, P1, K to end.
3rd round P1, K9, P3, *K2,
P2, rep from * to end.
4th round P1, K9, P1, K to
end.
Rep last 4 rounds until 12
more rounds have been
worked dec one st each side of
gussets every 6th round.
Next round P1, K5, P to end.
Rep last round once more.
Next round P1, K5, P1, K to
end.
Next round P1, K2 tog tbl,
K1, K2 tog, P1, K to end.
Next 2 rounds P1, K3, P to
end.
Next 2 rounds P1, K3, P1,
K to end.
Next round P1, K3, P to end.
Next round P1, K3 tog,
P to end.
Next round P3, K to end.
Next round P1, K1, P1, K
to end.
Next round P3, K2 tog tbl,
K to last 2 sts, K2 tog.
Next round P1, K1, P1, K
to end.
Next round P3, K to end.
Next round P1, K1, P1, K
to end.
Rep last 4 rounds until
57[61:61:65] sts rem.
Work until sleeve measures
15in or 3in less than desired
length, dec one st at beg of
last round.
Change to No.2 dp needles.
1st round *P1, K2, P1, rep
from * to end.
Rep 1st round until cuff
measures 3in.
Bind off in rib.

Blocking

Press lightly on wrong side
under a damp cloth using a
warm iron. Darn in ends
including joining first row ends
to complete lower edge circle.

Pretty and trim pants suit

Basic Wardrobe Knitting

Sizes

Directions are to fit 32in bust with 34in hips.
The figures in brackets [] refer to the 34, 36 and 38in bust sizes, and the 36, 38 and 40in hip sizes respectively.
Jacket. Length at center back, 27[27½:28:28½]in. Sleeve seam, 21[21:21½:21½]in.
Trousers. Inside leg seam, 29[30:30½:31½]in.

> **Gauge**
> 7 sts and 8 rows to 1in over st st worked on No.4 needles
> 8 sts and 8 rows to 1in over patt worked on No.4 needles

Materials

Reynolds Classique
Jacket. 4[5:5:6] 50 grm balls in dark color A
7[8:9:10] balls in light color B
7 buttons
Trousers. 11[12:13:13] balls in dark shade, A
One pair No.2 needles (or Canadian No.11)
One pair No.4 needles (or Canadian No.9)
Waist length of elastic

Pants left leg

**Using No.2 needles and A, cast on 160[166:174:180] sts and work 7 rows st st beg with a K row.
Next row K to form ridge for hemline.
Change to No.4 needles and continue in st st beg with a K row, until work measures 10[11:11½:12½]in from hemline, ending with a P row.

Shape leg

Next row K39[40:42:44], K2 tog tbl, K78[82:86:88], K2 tog, K39[40:42:44]. 158 [164:172:178] sts.
Work without shaping until leg measures 14[15:15½:16½] in from hemline, ending with a P row.
Next row K39[40:42:44], K2 tog tbl, K76[80:84:86], K2 tog, K39[40:42:44]. 156 [162:170:176] sts.
Work without shaping until leg measures 18[19:19½:20½]in from hemline, ending with a P row.
Next row K38[39:41:43], K2 tog tbl, K76[80:84:86], K2 tog, K38[39:41:43]. 154 [160:168:174] sts.
Work without shaping until leg measures 22[23:23½:24½]in from hemline, ending with a P row.
Next row K38[39:41:43], K2 tog tbl, K74[78:82:84], K2 tog, K38[39:41:43]. 152 [158:166:172] sts.
Work without shaping until leg measures 26[27:27½:28½]in from hemline, ending with a P row.
Next row K37[38:40:42], K2 tog tbl, K74[82:84:86], K2 tog, K37[38:40:42]. 150 [156:164:170] sts.
Work without shaping until leg measures 29[30:30½:31½] in from hemline, ending with a P row.
Mark center of last row with colored thread.

Shape front and back seams

Bind off 4 sts at beg of next 2 rows, then dec 1 st at each end of next 3 rows. 136[142: 150:156] sts. Work 1 row.
Dec 1 st at each end of next and every other row until 128 [134:142:148] st rem.
Work 7[9:9:11] rows without shaping.
Next row K2 tog, K60[63: 67:70], K2 tog tbl, K2 tog, K to last 2 sts, K2 tog. 124[130:138:144] sts.
Work 7 rows.
Next row K2 tog, K58[61: 65:68], K2 tog tbl, K2 tog, K to last 2 sts, K2 tog, 120[126:134:140] sts.
Work 5 rows.
Next row K2 tog, K56[59: 63:66], K2 tog tbl, K2 tog, K to last 2 sts, K2 tog. 116[122:130:136] sts.
Work 5 rows.
Continue dec in this way on next and every following 6th row until 88[94:102:108] sts rem.
Continue without shaping until work measures 9[9½:9½: 10]in from colored marker ending with a P row.**

Shape back

***1st row** K44[47:51:54], turn.
2nd and every other row P.
3rd row K33[35:38:40], turn.
5th row K22[23:25:26], turn.
7th row K11[11:12:12], turn.
9th row K across all sts picking up loop at point where work was turned and knitting it tog with next st to avoid hole.
Change to No.2 needles and work in K1, P1 rib for 1in. Bind off in rib.

Right leg

Work as for left leg from ** to **
Next row K.
Work as for left leg from *** to end, reading P for K and K for P.

Finishing

With WS facing, block each piece by pinning out around edges and omitting ribbing, press lightly using a cool iron and a dry cloth.
Using a flat seam for ribbing and a fine back-stitch seam for remainder, join front, back and leg seams.
Fold hems at hemline to wrong side and slip stitch hem in place. Work casing stitching inside waistband and thread with elastic. Press seams.

Jacket back

NB When working in stripe patt carry yarn not in use loosely along side of work.
Using No.2 needles and A, cast on 129[137:145:153] sts.
Work 5 rows garter st.
Change to No.4 needles, attach B and work in patt as follows:
1st row (RS) Using B, *K1, ytf, K2, sl 1, K2 tog, psso, K2, ytf, rep from * to last st, K1.
2nd row Using B, P.
Rep last 2 rows twice more.
7th row Using A, as 1st.
8th row Using A, as 2nd.
These 8 rows form patt.**
Continue in patt until Back measures 10in, ending with RS row. Change to No.2 needles and continue in patt until back measures 14in, ending with RS row.
Change to No.4 needles and continue in patt until back measures 20in, ending with RS facing.

Shape armholes

Keeping patt correct, bind off 3 sts at beg of next 2 rows, then dec 1 st at each end of every row until 109[117:125: 133] sts. rem.
Work 1 row.
Dec 1 st at each end of every other row until 97[101:105:109] sts rem.
Work without shaping until Back measures 27[27½:28:28½] in, ending with a WS row.

Shape shoulders

Bind off 9[9:9:10] sts at beg of next 4 rows, then 8[9:10:9] sts at beg of following 2 rows. Bind off rem 45[47:49:51] sts.

Left front

Using No.2 needles and A, cast on 65[69:73:77] sts. K 5 rows.
Change to No.4 needles, attach B and patt as follows:
1st and 3rd sizes only.
Work as for Back from ** to **.
2nd and 4th sizes only.
1st row (RS) Using B, *K1,

ytf, K2, sl 1, K2 tog, psso, K2, ytf, rep from * to last 5 sts, K1, ytf, K2, K2 tog tbl.
2nd row Using B, P.
Rep last 2 rows twice more.
7th row Using A, as 1st.
8th row Using A, as 2nd.
These 8 rows form the patt.
***All sizes** Continue in patt until Front measures 10in, ending with RS facing.
Change to No.2 needles and continue in patt until Front measures 14in, ending with RS row.
Change to No.4 needles and continue in patt until Front measures 20in, ending with same patt row as Back, ending with WS row.

Shape armhole and front edge
Next row Keeping patt correct, bind off 3 sts, patt to last 2[3:2:3] sts, K2[3:2:3] tog. 61[65:69:73] sts.
Next row P.
Dec 1 st at armhole edge on every row *at the same time* dec 1 st at neck edge on next and every other row until 50[54:58:62] sts rem.
Work 1 row.
Dec 1 st at each end of next and every other row until 38 sts rem.
Keeping armhole edge straight, continue dec 1 st at neck edge on every other row as before until 26[27:28:29] sts rem.
Work without shaping until Front measures same as Back to shoulder, ending with RS facing.

Shape shoulder
At armhole edge, bind off 9[9:9:10] sts every other row twice. Work 1 row.
Bind off rem 8[9:10:9] sts.

Right front
Using No.2 needles and A, cast

on 65[69:73:77] sts. K 5 rows.
Change to No.4 needles, attach B and work in patt as follows:

1st and 3rd sizes only.
Work as for Back from ** to **

2nd and 4th sizes only.
1st row (RS) Using B, K2 tog, K2, ytf, *K1, ytf, K2, sl 1, K2 tog, psso, K2, ytf, rep from * to last st, K1.
2nd row Using B, P.
Rep last 2 rows twice more.
7th row Using B, as 1st.
8th row Using B, as 2nd.
These 8 rows form patt.
Work as for Left front from *** to end, reversing shaping.

Sleeves
Using No.2 needles and A, cast on 50[52:54:56] sts and work in K1, P1 rib for 3½in.
Next row (Rib 1, pick up and K yarn before next st—called M1—) 2[5:2:5] times, *inc in next st, M1, rep from * to last 2[5:2:5] sts, (rib 1, M1) 1[4:1:4] times, rib 1. 145[145:157:

157] sts.
Change to No.4 needles, attach B and patt as follows:
1st row (RS) Using B, *K1, ytf, K4, sl 1, K2 tog, psso, K4, ytf, rep from * to last st, K1.
2nd row Using B, P.
Rep last 2 rows twice more.
7th row Using A, as 1st.
8th row Using A, as 2nd.
These 8 rows form patt.
Continue in patt until sleeve measures 12½in, ending with a WS row.

Shape sleeve sides
Next row *K1, ytf, K3, sl 2, K3 tog, p2sso, K3, ytf, rep from * to last st, K1. 121[121:131:131] sts.
Next row P.
Next row *K1, ytf, K3, sl 1, K2 tog, psso, K3, ytf, rep from * to last st, K1.
Keeping patt correct, rep last 2 rows until sleeve seam measures 16½in, ending with WS facing.
Next row *K1, ytf, K2,

sl 2, K3 tog, p2sso, K2, ytf, rep from * to last st, K1. 97[97:105:105] sts.
Next row P.
Next row *K1, ytf, K2, sl 1, K2 tog, psso, K2, ytf, rep from * to last st, K1.
Keeping patt correct, rep last 2 rows until sleeve seam measures about 21[21:21½:21½]in, ending with same patt row as Back before armhole shaping.

Shape cap
Bind off 3 sts at beg of next 2 rows.
Dec 1 st at each end of every other row until 73[65:73:65] sts rem.
Work 1 row.
Dec 1 st at each end of every row until 29 sts rem.
Bind off.

Finishing

Omitting garter st, block and press as for Pants. Join shoulder, side and sleeve seams.
Sew in sleeves.

Left front border
Using No.2 needles and A, cast on 11 sts.
1st row (RS) K2, (P1, K1) 4 times, K1.
2nd row (K1, P1) 5 times, K1.
Rep last 2 rows until border fits up Left front and around to center of Back when slightly stretched.
Bind off in rib.

Right front border
Work as for Left border working 7 buttonholes, first to come ½in above lower edge, 7th at start of neck shaping and remainder evenly spaced between.
First mark positions of buttons on Left front then work buttonholes as markers are reached.
Buttonhole row. (RS) Rib 4, bind off 3, rib to end.
On next row cast on 3 sts above those bound off.
Join borders at center back and stitch in position.
Press seams.
Sew on buttons.

1225

Introduction to hairpin crochet

Hairpin, or fork, crochet is so called because the main tool used resembles a long hairpin or tuning fork.

Types of hairpins or forks

In the past, these were made of steel and were like a square-ended letter U. They were rigid, a little heavy, and if different widths of work were required, a selection of different hairpins had to be used to allow for the variation. Nowadays, a hairpin frame is available which consists of two lightweight rods connected at top and bottom by plastic bars. By slotting the rods into different positions on the bars, the width can be altered.

Pattern making

There are two ways in which patterns can be created. Basically, all hairpin crochet consists of long strips joined together to form the finished article. The pattern can be given great variation in the center knot between each loop and also in the way in which the completed strips are joined.

Working single crochet

Because the frame is long it is best to work with both end bars on the rods, although the illustrations show the top bar removed. Without the top bar the loops tend to pull the rods together and gauge on the finished strip will not be even. Make a slip knot in the yarn and take the top bar off until you have placed the slip knot on the right-hand rod. Replace the bar. Draw the loop out so that the knot is exactly centered between the bars. Hold the

1226

yarn behind the left rod with the index finger and thumb of the left hand and turn the frame toward you from right to left until the right-hand rod has reversed to the left side. The yarn will now pass over the other rod and should be held again by the left hand behind the left-hand rod.

*Insert crochet hook through loop and draw a single thread through so that there are two loops on the crochet hook, yarn over hook and draw through both loops to complete one single crochet. Keeping loop on hook, pass the hook through to the back of the frame and turn the frame toward you from right to left as before. Repeat from *, turning the frame after each stitch. The frame is always turned the same way.

When the frame becomes full of completed loops, remove the bottom bar and slip most of the loops off the frame. Replace the bar and continue on remaining loops as before until the strip is the desired length.

To finish off, break the yarn and draw through the last single crochet.

Double single crochet

Work as for single crochet, working two single crochet instead of one by making the first into the loop as before and the second under both threads of the loop.

Single crochet on two threads

Work as for double single crochet but make both first and second single crochet under both threads of loop.

▲ *The slip knot loop on the frame*

▲ *The loop after turning the frame once*

▲ *Drawing the first loop through with a crochet hook*

▲ *Completing the first stage of the center stitch*

▲ *Completing the second stage of the center stitch*

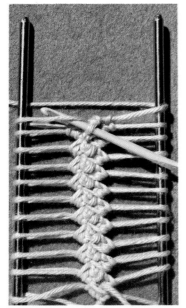

▲ *1st double single crochet stitch*

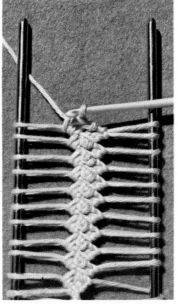

▲ *2nd double single crochet stitch*

▲ *1st stitch of dc on two threads*

▲ *2nd stitch of dc on two threads*

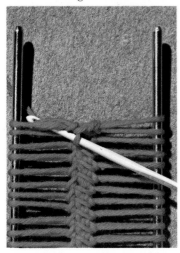

▲ *1st stitch of sc on two threads*
▼ *Joining strips with crochet hook*

▲ *2nd stitch of sc on two threads*

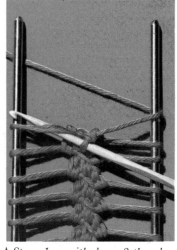

▲ *Stage 1 sc with dc on 2 threads*

▲ *Stage 2 sc with dc on 2 threads*
▼ *Joining strips with chain stitch*

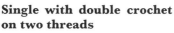

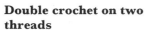

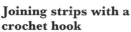

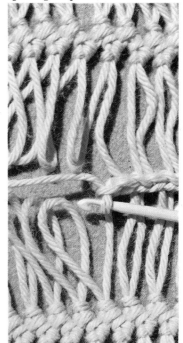

Double crochet on two threads

Work as for single with double crochet, making both stitches double and working them both under two threads of the loop.

Single with double crochet on two threads

Work as for double single crochet on two threads, making one single crochet under both threads of loop and then putting yarn over hook and working one double under both threads of loop.

Joining strips with a crochet hook

Place the two strips together horizontally. Using the crochet hook, lift one of the loops from the first strip and one from the second. Draw the second loop through the first then pick up the second loop of the first strip. Draw this through loop on hook then pick up second loop from second strip and draw the loop through. Continue in this way along the strips until they are joined together. Make sure that the final stitch is securely sewn to prevent it unraveling.

Joining with chain stitch

Place two strips together horizontally and work from right to left. Make a slip knot and place on crochet hook. *Insert hook through first loop of first strip and first loop of second strip, yarn over hook and draw through. Repeat from * until all the loops are joined, then finish off thread by drawing it through last stitch.

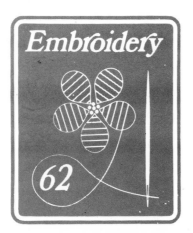

A modern interpretation of cut work

This modern interpretation of cut work embroidered in brilliant white on dark blue linen makes a striking decoration for a place mat and napkin holder. The embroidery would look equally attractive worked on any strong contrasting colored linen, or for a more traditional look work the embroidery in the same color as the fabric. The quantities for fabric and yarn are given for making one set only. For a set of six place mats and holders you will need $2\frac{3}{4}$ yards of linen and 48 skeins of yarn. Make or purchase a plain napkin to tuck into each holder. If you make the napkins, use one of the borders to decorate the edges.

To make a place mat measuring 12 inches by 18 inches and a table napkin holder measuring 5 inches by $10\frac{1}{2}$ inches.
You will need:
- ☐ 16 inches by 36 inches fine blue linen
- ☐ 8 skeins Snow white D.M.C. Brilliant Embroidery Cotton No. 25
- ☐ Blue sewing thread to match fabric
- ☐ Crewel needle No. 8

Preparing the fabric
Cutting on the straight of the material, cut one rectangle measuring 14 inches by 20 inches for the place mat and another rectangle measuring $12\frac{1}{2}$ inches by 15 inches for the table napkin holder.

Transferring the design
Trace the outlines of the place mat and the napkin holder design from these pages. Transfer these designs onto the fabric using white or yellow carbon paper, placing the borders one inch in from the cut edges.
Trace a single line to mark the top and bottom borders of the place mat. Trace a single line on the side edges of the napkin holder flap; the flap should measure 4 inches deep from the pointed edge of the border.

Working the design
The cutwork embroidery is worked entirely with Snow white Brilliant Embroidery Cotton No. 25. Embroidery chapter 56, page 1108, gives the instructions for preparing and working the buttonhole edging and buttonhole bars.
Work the pointed edge over 2 threads of the linen material taken as cord foundation.
Once the work is complete, press with a damp cloth, placing the right side of the material downward on a thick, soft pad.
Cut away the edges of the openwork. Press a second time on the wrong side of the work over a pad.
Finish the plain edges of the napkin folder by making a hand-sewn hem about $\frac{2}{5}$ of an inch wide.
Fold the napkin holder and close the side seams with small slip stitches.

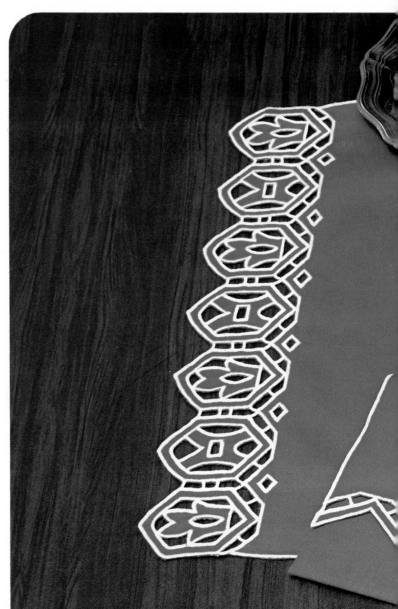

▲ *Crisp white cut work on dark linen makes a modern looking place mat and napkin holder to complement modern tableware.*

◄ *Actual size tracing design for half of the place mat border. The arrow head indicates the center of the border.*

Actual size tracing design for half of the napkin holder flap. The arrow indicates the center ►

Designs from fabrics and wallpapers

The repeat of the designs given in this chapter is marked on the tracing patterns in red outline.

Tracing a design

For this technique you will need a drawing board or a piece of soft board. Trace the design onto strong paper and outline it with India ink or a black felt-tipped pen. The outline must be solid enough for it to show through the canvas. Mark the center of the design with vertical and horizontal lines. Mark the center of the canvas in the same way with lines of basting stitches. Lay the design on a drawing board and, with thumbtacks, pin the canvas over the design, carefully matching up the center lines on canvas and design. Tilt the drawing board until the design shows through the canvas to the best advantage and paint the outlines with black water color paint and a fine paint brush using a slight scrubbing movement. For more simple designs, use a water-proof felt-tipped pen. Modern wallpaper and home furnishing fabric designs are equally adaptable to being translated into needlepoint. These needlepoint designs worked in tent stitch are reminiscent of the William Morris wallpaper and fabric designs which are enjoying renewed popularity today.

Try this waterlily design as a pattern for a pillow. For all-over patterns reverse

closed area on alternate rows

▼ A flower design which would look pretty worked as a rug

Running repairs to clothes

Turning a collar, making a new pocket, replacing lost buttons—all these repairs, properly done, will lengthen a garment's life and maintain its good looks.

Collars and cuffs

A shirt is one of the most worthwhile garments to repair. Usually, wear occurs on the collar and on the cuffs, and by turning the section or remaking the worn part the useful life of a shirt can be doubled.

Collars

Tailored shirt collars cannot be turned because there is an arrangement for bones or stiffening on the wrong side of the collar. Sports shirt collars can sometimes be turned. The method for turning these is the same as that given for turning double cuffs.

Remaking a shirt collar

Rip the collar from the shirt. Discard the worn collar surface and use the collar facing as a pattern to cut a new surface section. If necessary, cut a new interfacing too. Cut off the tail of the shirt, and from this fabric cut a new surface collar section, keeping the run of the grain correct and cutting a little extra seam allowance all around.

Stitch the interfacing to the wrong side of the collar facing, leaving the neck edge free. Trim the interfacing only, all around and across the corners, if a new interfacing is being used. With right sides facing,

1232

stitch the surface collar section to the collar facing and interfacing, leaving the neck edge open, stitching along the previous stitching line. Trim the corners and layer the seams where necessary. Turn the collar right side out and press, rolling the edges slightly to the underside so that the seamline does not show. Top stitch $\frac{1}{4}$ inch from the finished edge. Restitch the collar to the neckband and shirt. The shirt tail will have to be replaced, so use a piece of fabric of similar weight.

Turning and repairing double cuffs

Rip the cuff from the shirt sleeve, baste the pleat and regather the sleeve edge if necessary. If the wear is slight, darn the worn place with closely matching thread and replace the cuff with the darned part outside so that when the cuff is folded the darn is hidden. If the worn place cannot be darned satisfactorily, make a neat patch using a piece of fabric from the shirt tail. Replace the cuff the other way around so that the patched area is on the outside and is therefore hidden when the cuff is folded.

Repairing single cuffs

Rip the cuff from the sleeve. Regather the edge if necessary. Rip the cuff completely and cut away the worn edge. Remake the cuff and replace it on the sleeve. It will be shorter than it was before so both cuffs should be treated in the same way and the cuff edges trimmed back to the same depth.

Elastic waistbands

There is no rule of thumb for measuring the correct amount of elastic needed to go around a waist. It is best to try fitting a piece of elastic around the waist, stretching it until it fits but is still comfortable, before cutting a piece off. Allow 1 inch extra for overlapping the ends.

Men's and boys' shorts.

Waistband elastic for shorts is easily recognizable because it

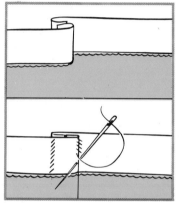

has an unelasticized edge. This is the edge which is attached to the garment. Rip the worn elastic from the shorts and iron out the gathered waist. Turn the edge in $\frac{1}{4}$ inch. Press. Measure and mark a piece of elastic into four and then eight parts. Measure and mark the waistband of the shorts into four and then eight parts. Place the elastic inside the garment so that the unelasticized edge is $\frac{1}{4}$ inch under the garment edge.

Match the marking on elastic and garment and pin vertically to the waistband at these points. Overlap the ends of the elastic and sew securely by hand (see diagram 1). Machine stitch two rows, $\frac{1}{8}$ inch apart, along the garment edge. The elastic will need to be stretched slightly as you stitch.

Replacing elastic in casing

If there is no opening in the casing, rip a few stitches so that the old elastic can be drawn out. Cut a new piece of elastic to the desired length plus 1 inch for overlapping the ends. Draw the elastic through the casing using a bodkin or a safety pin. Overlap and stitch

the ends securely. Restitch the casing closed.

Shoulder straps and ties

Broken shoulder straps, whether they are on lingerie, aprons or dungarees, are repaired by the same method.

If the garment is made of double material, as it is on some lingerie, rip the two layers and re-insert the strap deeply enough to prevent it from slipping out again.

Machine stitch or sew by hand, using a tiny backstitch, along the original stitching line.

If the strap is attached to a single thickness of fabric, turn $\frac{1}{8}$ inch of the strap end up and iron it. Place the strap in position so that the folded end is inside the garment, $\frac{3}{8}$ inch to 1 inch, depending on the thickness of the fabric and the size of the strap. Over-

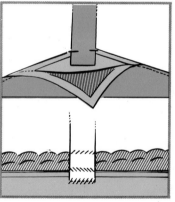

cast the folded edge of the strap, using small stitches, and again where the strap meets the edge of the garment. If, as in the case of lingerie, there is a lace edging, sew the strap to the edge of the lace too.

Repairing pockets

If the hole in the pocket is small and there is no surrounding worn area, a line of machine stitching across the pocket above the hole will usually suffice. If, however, the fabric is worn and thin, it is better to replace the pocket entirely. Pockets for pants, slacks and coats can be purchased, but if you prefer to make your own rip the old pocket from the garment and use it for a pattern. Heavy cotton makes the best pockets for heavy and medium weight garments, while lightweight cotton is best for children's clothes.

Inserting the pocket

Cut out two pieces of pocket and, placing them right sides facing, pin one pocket section to the front opening edge of the garment. Pin the other section to the back opening edge. Baste and then machine stitch from the bottom of the garment seam opening (marked A in the diagram) to B making a $\frac{3}{8}$ inch seam. Then stitch the

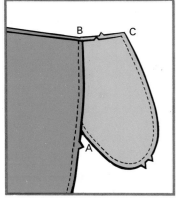

two pocket sections together from A to C, making a $\frac{5}{8}$ inch seam.

Buttons and buttonholes

If buttonholes become badly worn, there isn't much you can do to restore them except for turning them into bound buttonholes, matched with larger sized buttons. However, wear on buttonholes can be minimized by making sure that buttons are positioned properly so that there isn't too much strain on the buttonhole. Also make sure that the button has sufficient shank, or stem, so that there is space for the fabric between the button and the garment without causing undue strain. Some buttons are made with shanks, usually of metal, plastic or padded fabric. Shanked buttons are sewn onto garments using several strands, which are then finished off with loop stitch.

Stems for buttons

To make a thread shank or stem, a matchstick or three pins are placed across the button and the stitches are made over them. As the button is stitched on, the matchstick serves to

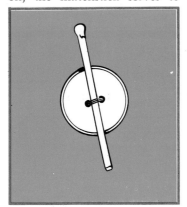

lengthen the stitches and this makes a basis for the stem.

To sew on a button neatly, make a backstitch on the wrong side and then pass the needle six to eight times through the button. It is important that the needle is passed through the fabric at the same spot each time so that an even bar of stitches is formed on the wrong side. When sufficient stitches have been made to hold the button, pass the needle through the button but not through the

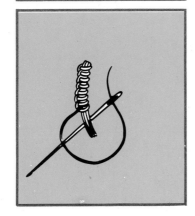

fabric. Wind the thread around the stem between button and fabric several times, and then pass the needle through to the inside of the garment.

After the shank has been completed, the bars on the inside of the garment should be finished off with loop stitching.

When working with four-holed buttons, work the stitches two holes at a time only, whether the stitches are intended to go diagonally, vertically or horizontally across the button, so that a strong bar of stitches shows for each two holes on the wrong side.

Stayed buttons

Buttons which receive extra strain or which are sewn to a single thickness of fabric should be reinforced. On the inside of the garment, directly under the button, place another smaller button or a small piece of tape and sew through the button, garment and reinforcing.

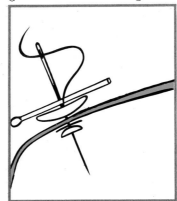

When a button has been accidentally pulled off and the fabric subsequently weakened, a piece of tape stitched invisibly inside the garment behind the button will strengthen the place so that the button can be replaced.

Buttons with unusually large holes can be attached to a garment with narrow ribbon, tape or cord. Cut a piece of tape 2 inches long. Thread the ends through the holes and tie a firm knot on the back of the button. Trim the ends of the tape, fold them under and whip them to the garment.

Repairing button loops

Measure the size of the button and make a mark for each

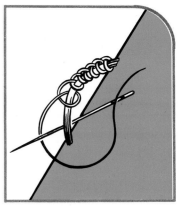

end of the button loop. Make a small backstitch on one mark and sew several long stitches between the two marks, taking up a single thread of fabric each time. Work close buttonhole stitch or blanket stitch over the strands. Fasten off with a double backstitch.

Binding worn edges

Binding can be successfully applied to worn coat and jacket edges, to cuffs, pockets and to worn edges of fur garments. Strips of leather in matching or contrasting colors can be used for furs and heavy garments, while braid and ribbon binding is used for other materials. To apply binding, make

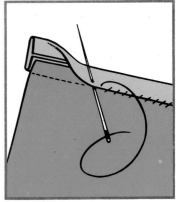

a line of small basting stitches, half the width of the binding, on the right side of the garment along the edge to be repaired. Baste the braid or binding, right side uppermost, along the basted line. Machine stitch (or hand sew, using whipping stitch) close to the edge of the binding. Fold the binding over the garment edge and hand sew down on the wrong side, working along the back of the machine stitching.

Collector's Piece

Embroidery is not a technique that can be used only to decorate tablecloths or enhance a dress. It can also be used to create beautiful pictures.

Painting with embroidery silks and cottons is no easy task—ask Mrs. Olga Pearce, a skilled dressmaker living in England. Two of her works appear on these pages; they have been chosen to illustrate the variety of effects to be achieved with a great deal of patience and no end of imagination.

As many embroiderers will realize, there are only four or five shades of each color to work with in embroidery materials.

This limitation makes it difficult to attain soft features in a portrait. But the main difficulty lies in transferring the preliminary sketch to canvas and retaining a likeness. Yet the artist has succeeded admirably in "Portrait of a Girl" *below*. Measuring 20in x 15in, this work contains 180,000 stitches in soft shades of gray. The photographic effect is heightened by the flat background and use of rather coarse stitches. Contrast the realistic treatment of this portrait with the cubistic style of the picture *opposite*, a detail taken from "Thai Dancers". The entire canvas

measures 29in x 18½in, and the other half of the picture is a mirror image of that shown here. There are 600 stitches to a square inch—a total of 320,000 stitches made with single threads of 6-strand floss. An extremely imaginative picture, it employs elements from many oriental cultures. The pagoda-like motif in the background, the slanted downcast eyes of the figures and their stylized postures are evocative of Thai temple dancers, while their tiered hats and flowing orange and saffron robes are reminiscent of Tibetan Lamas and Buddhist monks.

A fitted waist and a full skirt

This chapter deals with the particular fitting problems associated with a dress similar to pattern shown—the pattern comes with a fitted coat which is featured in the next chapter.

With the dress the reader is introduced to consequence fitting. Here each fitting point affects another and adjustments must be made in a certain sequence.

The Vogue Pattern has an unusual bodice line. The bodice darts have been dispensed with and the shaping taken into the bodice seam. While the particular application of the bodice muslin to check the bodice seams in this chapter only applies to similar seaming across the bust, a muslin is a useful guide to checking other fitted bodice styles.

Of general interest are the sections on fitting waist seams and full skirts. This information can be applied without complication to other full skirted and waisted styles, like the other dress on this page.

▲ *Vogue Pattern, back view*

▲ *Vogue dress pattern*

▲ *Full-skirted pattern*

Fabrics and linings

The fabric you choose for the Vogue Pattern, as for similar styled dresses, is very important. Firmly woven fabrics are not easily worked into molded styles, and the beginner is advised to choose a man-made fiber jersey—a fabric which has all the qualities required and in addition is shape-retaining and washable.

A softly molded style like this should be worn over a fitted slip and not have an attached lining. It is almost impossible to obtain the smooth finish required in a woven lining fabric and any fullness would make impressions through the fabric.

The dress with its bodice seam looks best in a plain fabric while the coat featured in the next chapter looks good in a patterned fabric, so look out for plain and patterned coordinating knits.

Checking the pattern

Before cutting out the fabric it is essential that you check the Front and Back bodice seams and skirt on the pattern as shown below. If you neglect these important fitting points, the whole garment could be useless through bad fitting which may be impossible to rectify once the garment has been cut out.

Checking the Front bodice seam

Since the darts have been taken into the shape of the Front and Back bodice seams, it is necessary that both seams are in the right position.

For a perfect pattern check, make a Front and Back bodice pattern as in figure 1, copying the muslin in Dressmaking 16, p. 316; or use

▲ *Vogue dress pattern*

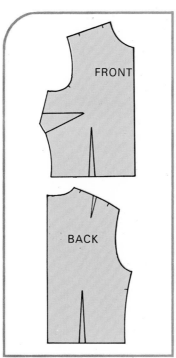

▲ **1.** *Bodice muslin pattern pieces*

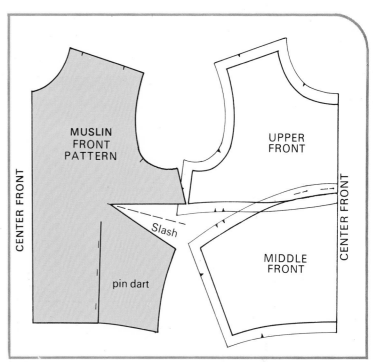

▲ **2.** *Preparing Front muslin pattern.* **3.** *Pinning the Front bodice seam*

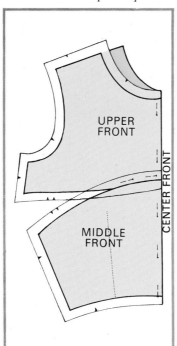

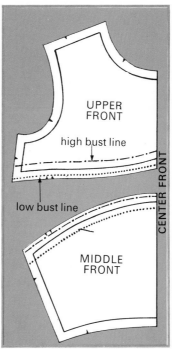

▲ **5.** *Alterations for high or low bust*

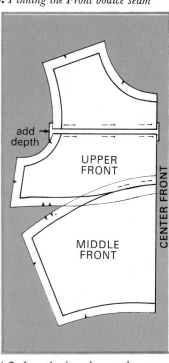

▲ **6.** *Lengthening above underarm*

the bodice of the corrected dress muslin pattern from Vogue 1004 (Dressmaking chapter 34, page 676).

Working on the muslin pattern, pin together the waist dart and slash the side bust dart along the center until the pattern lies flat (figure **2**).

Pin together the upper Front and middle Front sections of the Vogue pattern from the Center Front to where the seam curves (figure **3**).

Place the Vogue pattern over the muslin pattern and pin the Center Front edges together. The stitching lines and point of the side bust dart should be in line with the bodice seam as shown (figure **4**). If not, make the following adjustments:

i. Lower bustline. If the bustline on the muslin pattern is lower, compare the distances between shoulder and underarm lines on

both. If they are the same, shorten the middle Front section on the Vogue pattern by the required amount and add the amount taken away to the seamline on the upper Front section (figure **5**). Make sure you retain the original curve of the shaped seamline.

If the distance between shoulder and underarm line is greater on the muslin pattern, cut the Vogue upper Front pattern as shown (figure **6**), place over a strip of paper and spread by the required amount. After this correction the sleeve cap may also need to be adjusted slightly.

ii. Higher bustline. If the bustline on the muslin pattern is higher than that on the Vogue pattern, deduct the amount from the stitching line of the upper Front and add a corresponding amount to the stitching line of the middle Front (see figure **5**). Make sure you follow the original curve of the stitching line carefully.

iii. Full bustline. If your bustline is full, you may require more depth toward the ends of the bodice seams. You will see from the slant at the end of the dart lower stitching line if the dart on the muslin pattern is deeper than the dart incorporated into the Vogue pattern bodice seamline (figure **7**). The depth of the dart on the muslin is followed through into the curve of the waist seam.

Use the middle Front seamline edge to adjust the depth to correspond with the muslin pattern, and add to the waistline edge to compensate for the extra lift (figure **8**).

Adjusting for a fuller bust often results in the lower stitching line being longer than the upper stitching line on the muslin pattern. If so, add the extra length to the side seam of the middle Front section on the Vogue pattern.

Checking the Back bodice seam

If you have altered the position of the bodice seam on the Front of the Vogue pattern, raise or lower the Back bodice seam to correspond.

Now check the bodice seamline as it goes across the middle Back.

Pin the dart on the Back of the muslin pattern together. Pin the upper and middle Back sections of the Vogue pattern along the bodice seam from the Center Back toward the side seam to where the seam starts to curve.

Place the Vogue pattern over the muslin pattern and pin the Center Back edges together.

Slash the muslin pattern in line with the bodice seam (figure **9**). Check the amount by which it spreads, in order to lie flat, with the amount by which the seamlines of the upper and middle Back separate toward the side seam.

If you find that the spread of the muslin pattern is greater, make a small dart into the middle Back section of the Vogue pattern, as shown in figure **9**, until the distance of the slash lines and the seamlines is the same.

Checking the skirt

It is very important to check the width of a full skirt pattern before cutting to see that it hangs well. · It is not always possible to make adjustments after fitting as you may run out of length and be unable to make the alterations needed. The dart on the Vogue skirt pattern has been worked into the curve of the waist seam and the pattern has been spread to enable the fabric to fall in even folds around the skirt from hip to hem. With some figure shapes, this fullness tends to bunch at the side seams.

1238

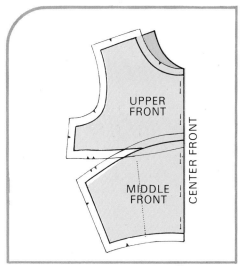

▲ **7.** *Checking pattern for full bust line·*

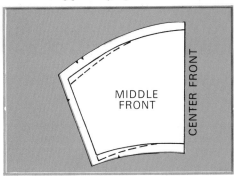

▲ **8.** *Correcting middle Front for a full bust*

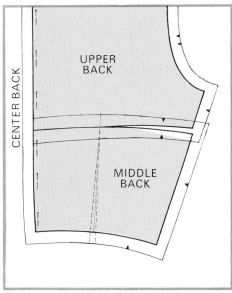

▲ **9.** *Checking the Back bodice seam*

The best way to check the Vogue pattern is to make and fit the basic skirt in Dressmaking chapter 4, page 76, then make a corrected basic skirt pattern incorporating your figure requirements and use this for checking the full skirt.

So, using the basic skirt pattern, pin the darts on the Back and Front and slash each pattern piece from the hem to the dart (figure **10**). Make another slash on each piece between the dart and center line

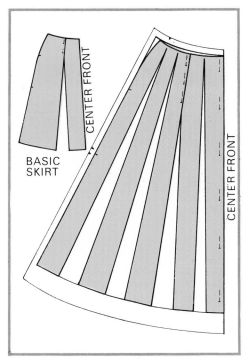

▲ **10.** *Preparing corrected basic skirt pattern*

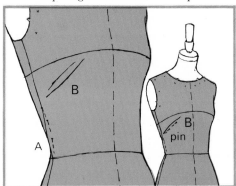

▲ **11.** *Pinning off diagonal fold on middle Front*

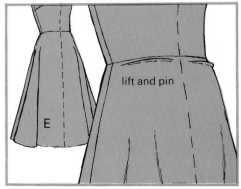

▲ **12.** *Pinning skirt for bunching at side seams*

from the hem to within ¼ inch of the waist and two more slashes between the dart and side seam, as shown.

Pin the center lines of each basic skirt pattern piece and the corresponding Vogue pattern piece together and spread the cut sections of the basic pattern until the hemlines meet at the side seams as shown.

Compare the waistline curve of the basic skirt with that of the Vogue pattern,

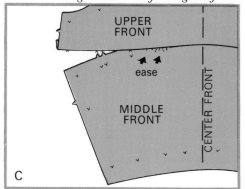

▲ 13. *Bunching at Front side seams only*

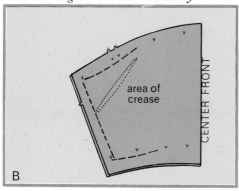

▲ 14. *Correcting middle Front for diagonal fold*

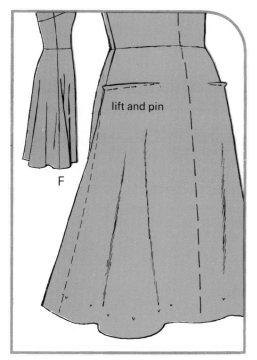

▲ 15. *Correcting the tight bodice seam*

making alterations to the waistline and side seams as necessary.

Cutting hints

On dresses with waist seams, cut extra deep seam allowances at the waist edge of both bodice and skirt pattern pieces as you may need to make further adjustments. For this style allow 1½ inches.

The bodice muslin pattern is always useful for checking the bodice fitting on waisted styles. If you have not made a bodice muslin and cannot check the pattern by this method, leave extra deep seam allowances on the bodice seam edges of the upper Front and Back.

On full skirts, cut an additional hem allowance so that you can make adjustments if necessary. Allow an extra 1½ inches for this style.

Fitting hints

Preparing for fitting
Follow the pattern step by step instructions to assemble the dress for fitting.

Waist fitting
To obtain an accurate waist fitting, pin and baste tape or soft belting to the waist seam of the dress. Cut it 2 inches longer than your waist measurement to allow 1 inch for ease and 1 inch for a wrap.

The secret of the good appearance of a waisted and full skirted dress lies in the fitting of the bodice—it should fit quite close to the body but not tightly.

Shoulders
To avoid a broad look across shoulders and hips, special attention must be paid to the fitting of the sleeves and they must be set into the armholes quite high on the shoulders.

Fitting the Vogue pattern

Memory fitting
There are some faults which cannot be corrected without ripping the side, waist and bodice seams. To rip these areas could spoil the correction of some other problem which can be dealt with fully at this stage. It is necessary therefore that you remember the fault which has occurred at a certain place, marking the spot with a pin so that you can deal with it later.

Follow the fitting sequences carefully and then make the necessary alterations following the same sequence.

Fitting the bodice
First check the fitting of the neckline and shoulders and proceed to the waistline, ignoring the bodice seam at this stage.

A. The middle Front section should fit closely over the midriff. Smooth out any fullness into the side seam.

B. After correcting A, you may be left

with a diagonal crease from the side seam towards the bodice seam (figure **11**). Pin off the depth of the crease and leave till later.

C. If you feel the dress is tight on the bodice seam as it passes over the height of the bust, mark the spot with a pin and correct later.

D. Make any necessary fitting corrections to the Back of the bodice.

Fitting the skirt
Before fitting the skirt, make sure that the waist seam fits closely but not tightly. The skirt should hang smoothly from the waist to the hips and then fall in soft folds toward the hem.

E. If you have not checked the waistline curve on the skirt against the corrected basic skirt pattern and the skirt bunches at the side seams, lift it a little on each side of the Center Front and Center Back to ease the fullness away from the sides. Pin the depth of the folds (figure **12**).

F. If you have a high seat but otherwise normal proportions, you will find that the skirt tends to bunch at the Front side-seams only. The bulk of your hip measurement is taken up around the Back and the width of the skirt Front must be reduced a little.

Lift the skirt into a small fold ½ inch deep, starting at each side seam and graduating to nothing toward the Center Front (figure **13**). Pin the fold.

The fullness in the skirt will then roll over the side seam toward the back. This indicates the amount by which to reduce the Front width.

Do not check the dress for length at this stage, but leave it until the waist seam has been stitched and the zipper inserted. Make all the fitting corrections you were able to follow through as usual, then work as follows.

Correcting the bodice
A. Taper side seams to take in fullness.

B. Rip the middle Front section from the upper Front and fold in half along the Center Front line. Pin. Measure the depth of the crease, and taper the bodice seam line by that amount (figure **14**).

To retain the correct length of the side seam, add the same amount to the waist seam as shown.

C. If you need a little more fullness over or under the bust, rip the side seams, and the bodice seams to within 2 inches of the Center Front on each side. Out of the side seam allowances, ease about ⅜ inch into the length of the lower Front bodice seam and carefully concentrate the extra ease over the height of the bust (figure **15**).

So that the seam allowance at the side seam is not short, lift the section which has been eased in slightly over the original seamline when you pin the bodice seam (figure **16**).

The lift should not be any more than $\frac{1}{4}$ inch at the side seamline tapering to nothing toward the bustline as shown. This will make the seam ends even again. The amount lifted into the bodice seam must be added to the side seam at the waist edge.

D. When making adjustments to the Back, make sure that you retain the good shape of the middle Back section which tapers slightly down towards the Center Back.

Remember. Always compensate for any adjustment you have to make. Although the shape changes to incorporate fitting details, the overall measurements or the width do not. For example: If you deduct from the middle bodice seam, this must be compensated for along the waist seam or the upper bodice seam. The exception is, of course, in the case of shortening, when the width of a section must be reduced right across. Always check the length of the side seams and make sure that the middle Front section and the middle Back section correspond so that the seamline is continuous around the bodice.

Correcting the skirt

If the hang of the skirt needs adjusting, rip the skirt completely.

E. If you have lifted the fullness away from the sides by pinning folds on the Front and the Back, it will be necessary to deepen the curve of the waistline as shown (figure **17a**).

Measure the depth of the fold then, working on the skirt pattern pieces, re-shape the waist seam by the required amount.

Increasing the curve will also increase the waist measurement, so make a dart at the waistline to the depth of the increase and pin (figure **17b**).

Use this pattern to recut the skirt.

F. If you had to ease the fullness out of the Front side seam only, pin a dart on the Front pattern $\frac{1}{2}$ inch deep and 5 inches down from the waistline on the side seam (figure **18a**).

Place the pattern Center Front to the straight edge of a sheet of paper and make a new pattern as follows.

Straighten the side seam, following the side seamline from the section above the dart to the hemline, so reducing the width of the skirt (figure **18b**).

Measure the distance between the edge of the paper and the original Center Front line of the pattern at the waist edge and take this away from the upper side-seam section as shown. Then deepen the waist curve by $\frac{1}{4}$ inch. This will make the waistline slightly larger but will be eased into the seam when making the dress.

Add the amount taken into the dart to the length of the hemline or the skirt will be too short (see figure **18b**).

Recut the skirt using the new pattern.

Making the dress

If you have made any of the above corrections, pin and baste the dress for a final fitting to insure that all is well.

When making the dress, follow the instructions given with the Vogue pattern until you come to the bodice seamline in step 12. When working on knitted man-made fiber fabrics, press the seam open and use a press pad when you reach the bust area of the seam. Use the contours of the seam and the fullness of the fabric on each side to guide you for shaping as you press.

If necessary, use a little steam while pressing, but don't use too much heat.

Continue with the instructions until you reach the waistline. If you finish the waistline with tape or soft belting, press the waist seam open to avoid bulk.

Finish the dress as shown and give it a final pressing.

▼ **16.** *Lifting eased section over original seam*

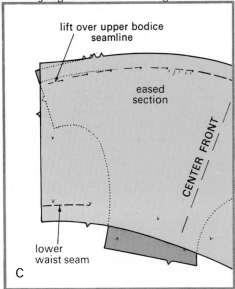

▼ **17.** *Correcting skirt pattern for bunching*

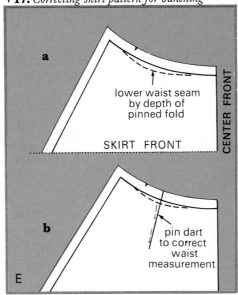

▼ **18.** *Correcting Front pattern for high seat*

Victorian nosegay

Trace the outlines of this nosegay design from the page and enlarge it to required size. Combined with border design shown in Embroidery chapter, p. 1250, it makes an

Pattern Library

attractive design for a table-cloth. The realistic effect is achieved by using six-strand floss in closely related tones worked in shaded long and short stitch. The stems are worked in outline stitch.

Introduction to embroidery on knitting

Knitting provides an ideal fabric for embroidery. It can be used either as a plain background for working random patterns, or the structure of the fabric can be used for counted thread types of patterns.

When decorating knitting, single stitches can be outlined in a contrast color to build up small motifs, as in Swiss darning. Alternatively, embroidery may be used to highlight a knitted pattern, a technique found in Tyrolean designs.

Swiss darning
Knitting a motif into the actual garment inevitably slows the process of knitting, and may present difficulties if rounded shapes are required. In such a case, the quickest method is to knit the garment in stockinette stitch and then to darn in the motif, by outlining the stitches of the motif-area. Thread the yarn into a darning needle and pass the needle through to the right side of the work at the base of a stitch. Draw the yarn through, leaving a short end at the back to darn in once the work is completed. Insert the needle behind the threads at the top of the same stitch, taking the needle through to the wrong side at the right-hand side of the stitch and out to the right side of the work at the left of the stitch. Then insert the needle back into the base of the same stitch. This will now have outlined one complete stitch and the process is repeated over all the necessary stitches. Run in both ends invisibly on the wrong side.

1242

Counted thread embroidery
In this technique, the upright and horizontal lines of the knitted stitch replace the canvas, and the spaces in the center of stitches or between stitches are used as holes.
It is best to use a darning needle with this method so that the knitted stitches are not spliced.

Tyrolean knitting
In these patterns the knitted stitches are used to create a self-colored pattern which is then highlighted by the addition of small, gay colored flowers, usually embroidered in wool. These are traditionally simple daisy shapes, sometimes formed by straight stitches like the spokes of a wheel, but more often with lazy-daisy stitch. These can be used to form leaves.

Tyrolean leaf pattern
The pattern is worked over 25 stitches and makes an attractive panel on either side of cardigan button panels.
1st row (RS) K6, P2 tog, P4, K up thread before next st tbl—called K up 1 tbl—, K1, K up 1 tbl, P4, P2 tog, K6.
2nd row K1, P4, K6, P3, K6, P4, K1.
3rd row K6, P2 tog, P3, (K1, ytf) twice, K1, P3, P2 tog, K6.
4th row K1, P4, K5, P5, K5, P4, K1.
5th row K1, sl next 2 sts onto cable needle and hold at back of work, K2, K2 from cable needle—called C4B—, K1, P2 tog, P2, K2, ytf, K1, ytf, K2, P2, P2 tog, K1, sl next 2 sts onto cable needle and hold at front of work, K2, K2 from

cable needle—called C4F—, K1.
6th row K1, P4, K4, P7, K4, P4, K1.
7th row K6, P2 tog, P1, K3, ytf, K1, ytf, K3, P1, P2 tog, K6.
8th row K1, P4, K3, P9, K3, P4, K1.
9th row K6, P2 tog, K4, ytf, K1, ytf, K4, P2 tog, K6.
10th row K1, P4, K2, P11, K2, P4, K1.
11th row K1, C4B, K1, P1, K1, P into front and back of next st twice, turn, K4, turn, P4, turn, K4, turn, sl 2nd, 3rd and 4th sts over first st then sl first st onto right-hand needle—called Bobble 1—, K1, P1, K1, C4F, K1.
12th row As 10th.
13th row K6, inc by purling into front and back of next st, K4, sl 1, K2 tog, psso, K4, inc in next st, K6.

14th row As 8th.
15th row K6, inc in next st, P1, K1, Bobble 1, K1, sl 1, K2 tog, psso, K1, Bobble 1, K1, P1, inc in next st, K6.
16th row As 6th.
17th row K1, C4B, K1, inc in next st, P2, K2, sl 1, K2 tog, psso, K2, P2, inc in next st, K1, C4F, K1.
18th row As 4th.
19th row K6, inc in next st, P3, K2 tog tbl, Bobble 1, K2 tog, P3, inc in next st, K6.
20th row As 2nd.
21st row K6, inc in next st, P4, sl 1, K2 tog, psso, P4, inc in next st, K6.
22nd row K1, P4, K7, P1, K7, P4, K1.
23rd row K1, C4B, K1, P13, K1, C4F, K1.
24th row K1, P4, K15, P4, K1.
These 24 rows form patt and are repeated as required.
(This pattern is not shown.)

▲ *A simple embroidery motif to trim mother's and daughter's outfits*

Outline Stitch --- Chain Stitch ●◉○ Beads

▲ *Diagram for embroidery in chain and outline stitches with beads*

▲ *Embroidered mittens and alternative knitted trim on red mitten*

Decorated mittens

Size

To fit an average adult hand
Length, about 10in.

Gauge

6 sts and 8 rows to 1in
over st st worked on No.
3 needles.

Materials

Reynolds Classique
Two·50grm balls
One set of 4 No.3 double
pointed needles
(or Canadian No.10)
Embroidery threads and beads

Left mitten

Using No.3 needles, cast on
48 sts and divide on 3 needles.
Cuff round *K1 tbl, P1, rep
from * to end.

Rep this round until cuff
measures 3in.
Change to st st.
1st round K22, lift thread
before next st and K into back
of it to M1 (this becomes
center st of thumb gusset), K26.
2nd round K.
3rd round K22, M1, K1,
M1, K26.
4th round As 2nd.
5th round K22, M1, K3,
M1, K26.
6th round As 2nd.
Continue in this way until
there are 19 sts on thumb
gusset. 67 sts.

Divide for thumb

1st round K22, sl next 19
sts onto thread or holder and
leave for thumb, K26.
Continue around on 48 sts
until work measures 9in from
cast-on edge or desired
length to tip shaping.

Shape tip

1st round *K2, K2 tog, K17,
sl 1, K1, psso, K1, rep from *
once more.
2nd round *K2, K2 tog,
K15, sl 1, K1, psso, K1, rep
from * once more.
Continue dec in this way on
every round until 4 sts rem.
Break yarn and draw through
rem sts and fasten off.

Thumb

Divide 19 sts from holder onto
3 needles. K 1 round.
2nd round K1, *K2 tog, K7,
rep from * once more. 17 sts.
Work for 2in without shaping.

Shape thumb tip

1st round *K2, K2 tog, rep
from * to last st, K1.
2nd round *K1, K2 tog, rep
from * to last st, K1.
3rd round K1, *K2 tog, rep
from * to end. Break yarn and

draw through rem sts. Fasten
off.

Right mitten

Work as for Left mitten, reversing position of thumb by working gusset after 26 sts instead
of 22 sts.

Finishing

Press mittens under a damp
cloth with a warm iron,
omitting ribbing.
Embroider back as in diagram.

Alternative knitted trim
Using No.3 needles, cast on
120 sts.
K 1 row. P 1 row. Bind off.
Allow strip to curl so cast-on
and bound-off edges touch.
Slip stitch together if preferred
to give a firm finish. Curl
strip to form a design.

Matched pullovers in Fair Isle

Sizes

Ladies. Directions are for 36in bust.
The figures in brackets [] refer to the Ladies 38 and 40in sizes respectively.
Length at center back, 21[22: 23]in, adjustable.
Sleeve seam, 18[19:20]in, adjustable.

Men's. Directions are for 38in chest.
The figures in brackets [] refer to the Men's 40 and 42in sizes respectively.
Length at center back, 23½ [24½:25½]in, adjustable.
Sleeve seam, 17½[17½:18]in, adjustable.

Gauge

6 sts and 8 rows to 1in over st st worked on No.4 needles
6½ sts and 8½ rows to 1in over st st worked on No.3 needles

Materials

3-ply fingering yarn
Ladies. 7[8:9] 1oz balls main color A, coral
1 ball each of 5 colors B, C, D, E and F, white, gray, dark brown, beige and medium brown
One pair No.3 needles (or Canadian No.10)
One pair No.4 needles (or Canadian No.9)
One circular needle No.4
4 small buttons
One large stitch holder
One No.D (3.00 mm) crochet hook
Men's. 8[9:9] 1oz balls main color A, natural
2 balls 1st contrast B, white
1 ball each of 4 colors C, D, E and F, gold, medium brown, dark brown and camel
One pair No.4 needles (or Canadian No.9)

One pair No.3 needles (or Canadian No.10)
One set of 4 No.4 double point needles

Circular yoked sweater

Front

Using No.3 needles and A, cast on 113[117:121] sts.
Work 4in K1, P1 rib.
Change to No.4 needles
Work in st st, beg with a K row and inc one st at each end of 7th and every following 8th row until there are 121 [127:133] sts.
Continue without shaping until work measures 14[14½: 15]in or length required, ending with a P row.

Shape armholes

Bind off 6 sts at beg of next 2 rows.
Dec one st at each end of next and every other row until 103 sts rem. P 1 row.

Shape for yoke

1st row K2 tog, K33, K2 tog, slip rem 66 sts on holder. Continue on 35 sts for left side.
Dec one st at each end of every K row until 3 sts rem.
Last row K2 tog, K1. Bind off.
With RS facing, slip first 29 sts onto holder for yoke and attach yarn to rem 37 sts. Finish to match other side.

Back

Using No.3 needles, cast on 112[116:120] sts and work as for Front, noting that there is one st less. When shaping for yoke, leave only 28 sts instead of 29 sts on holder.

Sleeves

Using No.3 needles, cast on 60[62:64] sts.
Work 4in K1, P1 rib.
Change to No.4 needles.
Continue in st st beg with a K row, inc one st at each end of 5th and every following 6th row until there are 84[90:96] sts.
Work until sleeve measures 18[19:20]in or desired length (allowing 2in for turn back cuff), ending with a P row.

Shape cap

Bind off 6[6:8] sts at beg of next 2 rows.
Dec one st at each end of every K row until 36 sts rem.
Slip sts on holder for yoke.

Yoke

Sew up raglan seams.
With RS facing, slip first 14 sts of Back onto holder.
Beg from center Back with A and first double pointed needle, pick up and K rem 14 sts of Back, pick up and K31[34:37] sts from raglan side, K36 sts from sleeve holder, using 2nd needle, pick up and K31[34:37] sts from next raglan side, K29 sts from Front holder, pick up and K31[34:37] sts from next raglan side, using 3rd needle K36 sts from 2nd sleeve, pick up and K31[34:37] sts from last raglan side and 14 sts from center Back. 253[265: 277] sts.
Using A, P 1 row. Attach F.
Next row *K3A, 1F, rep from *, ending 1A.
Next row *P1F, 1A, rep from * ending 1F.
Next row K1A, *1F, 3A, rep from * to end of row. Break off F.
Using A, P 1 row. Break off A.
Using B, K 1 row. P 1 row.
Continue working from chart.
1st size Skip first 6 sts of chart 1. Work rem 19 sts of chart 1, K40 sts of both charts 2 and 1 five times, then the 15 sts of chart 2 once, ending round with first 19 sts of chart 1.
Continue with rem 24 rows of charts, beg K rows from 7th st and P rows from 19th st at front edge of garment. Dec on chart on 9th and every other

▼ *Star and tapered star motifs for yoke.* *Tapered stars alternate with stars*

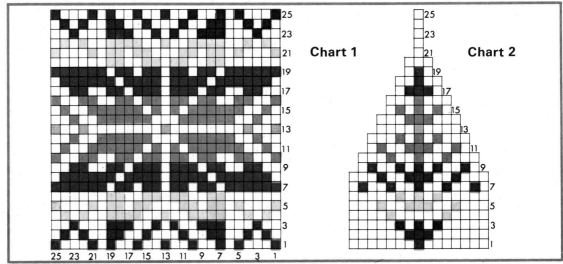

Chart 1

Chart 2

1244

row is worked by K2 tog tbl.
*After completing 25 chart rows using B, P 1 row.
Next row *K1, K2 tog, rep from * to end of row. Break off B.
Using A, P 1 row.
Next row *K3A, 1F, rep from * to end.
Next row *P1F, 1A, rep from * to end.
Next row K1A, *1F, 3A, rep from * to end. Break off F.
Using A, P 1 row.
Next row *K2, K2 tog, rep from * to end of row. P 1 row.
Change to No.3 needles.
Work 1in K1, P1 rib. Bind off loosely in rib.*

2nd size Work from chart, K from 1st row of chart 1 followed by 1st row of chart 2 across 11 sts, ending with 25 sts from chart 1, noting that dec on 9th and every other row is made by K2 tog tbl. Complete from * to * as for 1st size.

3rd size Work as for 2nd size, working every row with 6 sts in B before and after sts from charts.

All sizes Sew up Back opening leaving 4½in open. Crochet 1 row sc around both opening edges. Work 2nd row sc on RS making 4 loops for buttonholes.

Banded sweater

Back

Using No.3 needles, cast on 115[121:127] sts. Work 1½in K1, P1 rib.
Change to No.4 needles. Work in st st beg with a K row until work measures 11[11½:11½]in, ending with a P row.
Continue in st st, working 39 rows from chart. If desired, continue in st st until work measures 15½[16:16]in or desired length, ending with a P row.

Shape armholes
Bind off 6 sts at beg of next 2 rows.
**Next row K1, K2 tog, K to last 3 sts, sl 1, K1, psso, K1.
Next row P.**
Rep last 2 rows until 37[39:41] sts rem, ending with a P

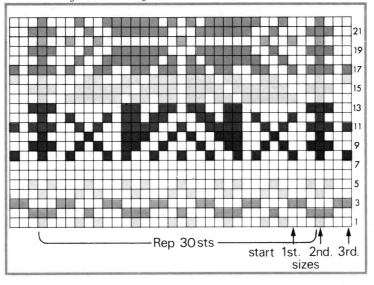

▼ *Bottom half of banded sweater motif. Work rows 19 to 1 for top half. The whole of the star motif is worked over 39 rows*

Rep 30 sts — start 1st. 2nd. 3rd. sizes

row. Slip sts on holder.

Front

Work as given for Back until 57[59:61] sts rem, ending with a P row.

Shape neck
1st row K1, K2 tog, K17, turn and leave rem sts on holder.
2nd row P to end.

3rd row K1, K2 tog, K to last 3 sts, sl 1, K1, psso, K1. Rep 2nd and 3rd rows 6 times more, then 2nd row once.
Next row K1, K3 tog, K1.
Next row P3.
Next row K1, K2 tog.
Next row P2 tog and fasten off.
With RS facing, slip first 17 [19:21] sts onto holder. Attach yarn to rem sts, K to last 3 sts, sl 1, K1, psso, K1.

Complete to correspond to other side.

Sleeves

Using No.3 needles, cast on 47[49:51] sts and work 3in K1, P1 rib.
Change to No.4 needles. Continue in st st beg with a K row, inc one st at each end of 5th and every following 6th row until there are 85[89:93] sts. Work until sleeve measures 19[19:19½]in or required length, ending with a P row. Place a marker thread at each end of last row. Work 8 rows more.

Shape cap
Rep from ** to ** as for Back until 47 sts rem, ending with a P row.
Next row K1, (K2 tog, K18, sl 1, K1, psso, K1) twice.
Continue to dec in center of every 6th row 4 times more, *at same time* dec at each end of every K row until 9 sts rem, ending with a P row. Slip sts on holder.

Neckband

Join raglan seams, sewing last 8 rows of sleeve cap above marker threads to bound-off sts at armhole.
Using No.3 needles and with RS facing, K across sts of right Sleeve, Back neck and left Sleeve, knitting 2 tog across each raglan seam, pick up and K14 sts down Front neck, K Front sts and pick up and K14 sts up other side of neck. 98[102:106] sts.
Work 2½in in K1, P1 rib. Bind off loosely in rib.

Finishing

Yoked sweater
Sew up side and sleeve seams. Sew on buttons to correspond to loops. Press with a damp cloth and warm iron, omitting ribbing.

Banded sweater
Join side and sleeve seams. Fold neckband in half to wrong side and slip stitch in place. Press with a warm iron over a damp cloth.

Pillow to make in hairpin crochet

Once you have mastered the basic principles of hairpin crochet, you can progress to more complex groupings such as those explained in this chapter. Designs in hairpin crochet are made by joining long strips of loops together. The method used to anchor the stitches as they are made can vary, but the joining of the loop stitches is what gives each design its originality. The designs featured here are fan shaded and peacock tail.

Fan shaded grouping

Work 3 strips of hairpin crochet using sc on 2 threads (see Crochet Know-how chapter 62, page 1226).

Before joining the strips, work 1 row sc along each side as follows:

1st side *Work 1sc into group of 20 loops, work 1sc into each of next 20 loops, rep from * to end.

2nd side *Work 1sc into each of next 20 loops, work 1sc into group of next 20 loops, rep from * to end.

The strips will now be curved instead of straight and are ready to join together with crochet.

Attach yarn to first st at right side of first strip with ss. Work ch5, work 1sc into 2nd st of left side of 2nd strip, *ch5, 1sc into 3rd st from last st on 1st strip, ch5, 1sc into 3rd st from last st on 2nd strip, rep from * until strips are joined together. Other strips are joined in the same way.

Peacock tail grouping

Work strips as for preceding
1246

design, working the edge grouping as follows:

1st side *(Work 1sc into group of 8 loops) 5 times, twisting loops over so that they lie as shown in the illustration, work 1sc into next 20 loops twisted, rep from * to end.

Work 2nd side in same way, arranging the 20-looped groups so that they come in the center of the five 8-loop groups. When the stitches are grouped, join the strips in the same way as for Fan grouping, or slip st edges tog.

Hairpin crochet pillow

Size

About 14in diameter.

> **Gauge**
> Worked on a Hairpin Lace Frame measuring about 2¾in from outer edges.

Materials

3-ply fingering yarn
2 ounces color A, lilac
1 ounce color B, purple
One Hairpin Lace Frame
One No.F (4.00 mm) crochet hook
One No.B (2.00 mm) crochet hook
Darning needle
Small safety pins
Foam rubber form

Front

1st strip for center

Using color A and No.B crochet hook, work strip of 66 loops at either side of center stitches worked in double single crochet (see Crochet Know-how chapter 62).

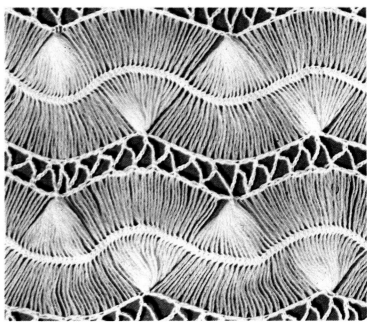

▲ *Fan shaped grouping*

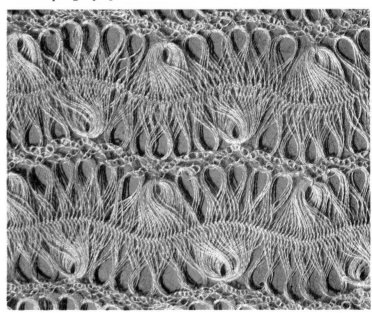

▲ *Peacock tail grouping*

Fasten off ends, joining first and last center stitches together so that strip forms a circle. Thread darning needle with short length of A and thread through the inner side loops of strip. Draw up to form center of pillow and fasten off ends securely.

2nd strip

Using B, work as for 1st strip until there are 132 loops at either side of middle stitches. Fasten off. Join first and last stitches so that strip forms circle.

Join 1st and 2nd strips

Using No.B crochet hook,

work the two strips together. Slip 2 loops from first strip onto hook, slip 4 loops from second strip onto hook and draw through first 2 loops. Slip next 2 loops from first strip onto hook and draw through loops already on hook, slip next 4 loops from second strip onto hook and draw through loops on hook. Continue in this way until all loops are joined. Thread a piece of yarn through last group and sew in place.

Leave loops on other side of 2nd strip grouped ready for next joining row. Slip 12 loops onto a safety pin. Repeat

Back

Using B and No.B crochet hook, ch7. Join into circle with ss into first ch.

1st round Ch7, (1tr in circle, ch3) 7 times. Join with a ss into 4th of first 7ch.

2nd round Ss to center of ch loop, ch7, (1tr in next ch loop, ch3, 1tr in same loop, ch3) 7 times. Join with a ss into 4th ch.

3rd round Ss to center of ch loop, ch7, (1tr in next loop, ch3, 1tr in same loop, ch3, 1tr in next loop, ch3) 7 times. Join with a ss into 4th ch. 21tr.

Continue in rounds in this way, working 2tr into a ch sp where an increase is required, spacing the number of increases evenly around the circle.

Work so that next round has 28tr.

5th round Has 40tr.
6th round Has 45tr.
7th round Has 48tr.
8th round Has 54tr.
9th round Has 62tr.
10th round Has 68tr.
11th round Has 74tr.
12th round Has 78tr.
13th round Has 86tr.
14th round Has 94tr.
15th round Has 98tr.
16th round Has 104tr.
17th round Has 116tr.
Fasten off.

Joining Front and Back

Place Back on top of Front, right sides out. With Back facing, insert No.B crochet hook through ch loop of Back and draw through 2 loops from edge of 4th Front strip, insert hook into next ch loop of Back and draw through next 2 loops from 4th strip, drawing them through 2 loops already on hook. Continue in this way until three quarters of the way around pillow. Insert form and continue until all the loops are joined through the Back ch loops. Fasten the last loops securely with a thread. Make a tassel with A, about 8in long, and attach to center.

▲ *Pillow worked combining both methods of joining strips, with and without additional threads*

until all loops are on pins (11 groups in all).

3rd strip

Using A, work strip as for 1st strip until there are 176 loops at either side of middle stitches. As the strip lengthens, place loops onto safety pins in groups of 16. This makes counting and joining simpler. Fasten off ends and join first and last middle stitches together, forming circle.

Join 2nd and 3rd strips

Using A and No.F crochet hook, join with 1sc to middle stitches of 2nd strip between two groups of 12 loops. 1sc into all 16 loops of first group on 3rd strip removing safety pin, *ch11, 1sc into middle sts on 3rd strip before second group of 16, 1sc into next group of 12 loops on 2nd strip removing pin, ch11, 1sc into middle sts on 2nd strip before next group, 1sc into next group of 16 loops on 3rd strip, rep from * until all loops are joined, completing circle with 1ss into first sc.

4th strip

Using B, work as for 1st strip until there are 232 loops on either side of middle sts, slipping loops off frame in groups of 8 on safety pins for next joining row. Fasten off ends, joining first and last middle sts to form circle.

Join 3rd and 4th strips

Using No.B crochet hook, slip 3 loops from 3rd strip onto hook, slip 4 loops from first safety pin of 4th strip onto hook and draw through loops already on hook, slip next 3 loops from 3rd strip onto hook and draw through loops, slip next 4 loops from 4th strip onto hook and draw through loops. Continue in this way until all loops are joined, securing last group with thread.

1247

Collector's Piece

These charming crewel work panels were designed by Erica Wilson, a graduate of the Royal School of Needlework, who was invited to America in 1954 to instruct the Needlework Guild of Millbrook, New York.

She has lived in America ever since, and Erica Wilson designs are now well-known and loved by embroiderers all over the United States. Erica Wilson's designs, of which there are now many hundreds, cover a wide variety of subjects: formal still lifes of flowers and fruit, casual groups of field flowers, seascapes, landscapes, birds and mythical beasts, cottages and farmhouses, and some delightful little story book pictures from children's books and poems. All her designs have a charming simplicity which encourage even beginners to try their hand at crewel wool embroidery, and the gaiety and ebullience of the designer herself lives in her designs. Erica Wilson uses embroidery stitches in a way which shows her complete familiarity with the techniques of her craft. She makes a few simple stitches work hard, varying their effect in unorthodox ways. The sails of the Nantucket whaling ship, for instance, consist of very long, uncouched strands achieving the look of wide stretches of canvas; long stitches are used again for the grass in the foreground of the farmhouse picture, but this time the designer has couched down the strands with chain stitch to alter the effect and break up what would have been a large area of color.

Erica Wilson is the author of *Crewel Embroidery, Fun with Crewel Embroidery* and *The Craft of Crewel Embroidery.*

Top left: "Blossoming springtime on the farm". Original size 9 inches by 11 inches.
Left: "Blazing glory". Original size 22 inches by 18 inches.
Right: "Nantucket whaler". Original size 20 inches by 24 inches.

All designs are the copyright of Erica Wilson/ Columbia-Minerva Corporation, USA.

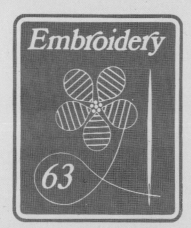

Inspired by beautiful chinaware

It isn't necessary to be an artist to create designs for embroidery—there are good designs around us, just waiting to be used. The print on wallpaper or home furnishing fabric, for instance, or the pattern on fine quality china, can be interpreted into embroidery stitches.

The beautiful designs in this chapter have been adapted from the pattern on a Josiah Wedgwood dinner service called "Plain Patrician". The success of the interpretation lies in the choice of embroidery stitches used. For example, the table-cloth border has been worked in stitches which duplicate the raised, sculptured texture of the plate edge, and the flower motif in stitches which can reproduce shading.

To embroider the cloth illustrated

Make or purchase a circular cloth measuring 72 inches across, and make or purchase a set of napkins to match. To make a cloth and set of napkins you will need 3¼yds 80 inch wide cotton and Dacron even-weave embroidery fabric in white. If you decide to make a cloth, embroider the edge with padded buttonhole scallops (see Embroidery chapter 10, page 190).

Transferring the design

Trace the border and napkin designs from these pages and transfer them to the fabric, as described in Embroidery chapter 4, page 68. Enlarge the flower design as described in Embroidery chapter 16, page 286, or trace a design from your own china.

▲ Tablecloth showing an arrangement of border and flower designs

Stitches and thread used

The flower design is worked in shaded long and short stitch and outline stitch. The delightful sculptured effect of the border is achieved by working in white thread on white fabric and using a combination of double backstitch, padded satin stitch, raised outline bands, long and short stitch and Russian filling. The embroidery is worked in six-strand floss using three strands in the needle.

▲ *"Plain Patrician" pattern from which the designs are taken*

▲ *The flowers on a napkin*   ▼ *Border to trace and enlarge*

Clever cat hand puppets

It would be difficult to find a more charming pair of pets than Percy and Prudence. These hand puppets are simple to make. You may find you already have some fabric remnants you can use—Percy and Prudence don't ask for much! The patterns are opposite.

Percy

You will need

For the puppet:
- ☐ ¾yd 36in wide corduroy or needlecord
- ☐ ¼yd 36in wide yellow cotton poplin
- ☐ ½yd 1½in wide ribbon
- ☐ Kapok to stuff the head (1oz is enough for each puppet)
- ☐ Scraps of gray, pink and brown felt
- ☐ Matching sewing thread, basting thread
- ☐ Pins
- ☐ Red embroidery floss, embroidery needle
- ☐ Plastic thread for the whiskers
- ☐ 12in yellow bias binding

For pattern making:
- ☐ A sheet, at least 20 inches square, of squared paper (1in squares). Either rule up brown paper or use graph paper
- ☐ Pencil
- ☐ Scissors

Making the pattern

Copy all the pattern pieces and their markings from the graph onto the squared paper, one square on the graph being equal to one 1in square on the paper.

Cut out the pattern pieces around the edges (the pattern includes seam allowance).

Cutting out

Fold the corduroy in half, right sides facing, and pin the side head, back head, body and ear pieces to the folded fabric. Cut out 2 body pieces, 2 side head pieces, 2 back head pieces and 2 ears. Unpin the ear pattern piece, repin it to the rest of the folded fabric and cut out 2 more ears.

Unfold the corduroy, pin the center head pattern piece to the single thickness of fabric and cut out.

Mark with basting thread all the seamlines and other pattern details.

Pin the nose pattern and the eye pattern piece A to the gray felt scraps and cut out 1 nose and 2 eye pieces.

From the pink felt cut 2 eyes, B, and from the brown felt 2 eyes, C.

Fold the cotton poplin in half and pin on the jacket pattern pieces, placing the center back line on the fold. Cut out 2 jacket fronts and 1 jacket back. Mark all seamlines with basting thread.

Making the puppet

Place the two body pieces together, right sides facing, and stitch from A to C to D to B. Trim the corners and snip into the seam allowance on the curves. Turn right side out and make a turned hem on the lower edge.

Place the two side head pieces together, right sides facing, and stitch from G to F. Insert the center head piece between the side pieces matching MG, OH and NH and stitch into position, right sides facing.

Place the two back head pieces together, right sides facing and stitch from K to J.

Stitch the ears together in pairs, leaving Q to R open. Trim the seams, snip into the curves and turn right side out.

Pin the ears into position on the right side of the front head, with the point of each ear pointing downward and the dot level with the seam at OH and NH respectively.

With right sides facing pin the back head section into position with the points L to the points E and with J to the center between the ears. Stitch.

Pin the nose into position where the side and center head pieces meet and sew around the edge with tiny invisible stitches. Take the three eye pieces, place C on B on A and stab stitch them together through the center. Position them on the side head pieces and sew around each eye with tiny stitches.

Make French knots on each side of the nose with red embroidery floss.

Cut 4 short lengths of plastic thread, each 4½ inches long. Sew two pairs of whiskers on

▲ *Prudence and Percy are two little kittens without any mittens!*

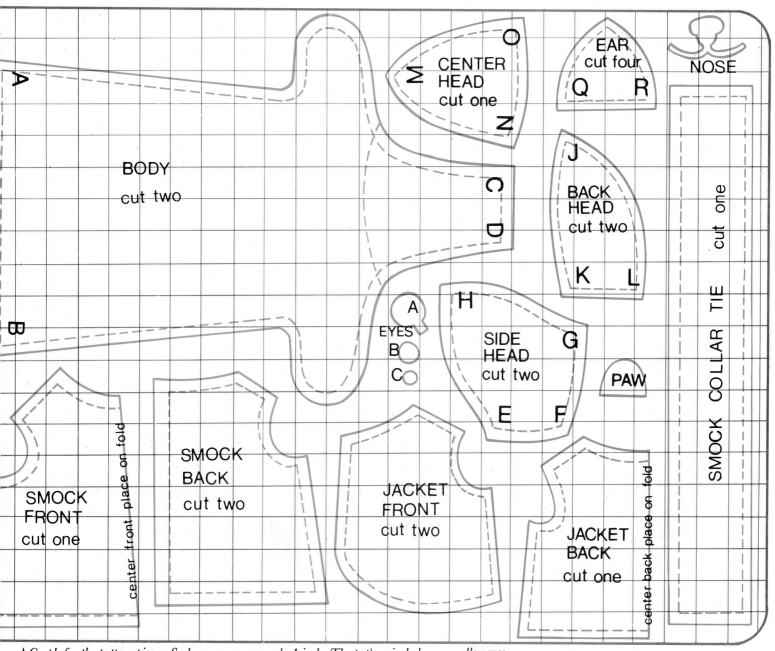

A *Graph for the pattern pieces. Scale: one square equals 1 inch. The pattern includes seam allowance*

each side of the nose, taking each length of plastic thread through the fabric in a small stitch and then securing it close to the fabric with a knot.

Insert a little kapok into the head. Turn under the neck edge and baste. Position the head over the body by putting your hand inside the body with the first two fingers in the neck section and pin the head into place.

Sew the head to the body with firm stitches around the neck edge, easing in any surplus.

The jacket. Place the jacket fronts to the jacket back, right sides facing, and stitch the shoulder and side seams. Hem around the edges of the jacket and the neckline. Bind the armholes with bias binding. Make a bow from the ribbon and sew it to the center front of the jacket when the jacket is on the puppet.

Prudence

You will need

- [ ] ¼yd 54in wide jersey
- [ ] ¼yd white cotton piqué
- [ ] Kapok (as for Percy)
- [ ] Scraps of brown and pink felt
- [ ] Matching sewing thread, basting thread
- [ ] Red embroidery floss, embroidery needle
- [ ] Pins
- [ ] Plastic thread
- [ ] Pattern making materials as for Percy

Make a pattern as before.

Cut the body and head pieces from jersey. Cut the nose, paws and eye pieces A and C from brown felt. Cut eye piece B from pink felt.

Making the puppet

Make the puppet in the same way as Percy. The only details to add are the paws—sew them on after you have attached the eyes and nose.

The smock. From the white cotton piqué cut 2 back pieces and 1 front piece, center front to fold. Cut 1 collar tie, mark the seamlines with basting.

With backs and front together, right sides facing, stitch the side and shoulder seams. Hem down each side of the center back along the lower edge and around the armholes.

Place the tie, right sides facing, to the neck edge, making sure there is an equal amount on either side of the back opening for tying. Stitch around the neck. Turn the tie to the wrong side, slip stitch along seamline, make the ends neat.

Lampshade and pillow in macramé

Two more fascinating macramé projects; a lampshade using decorated square knots and a modern-looking pillow in Teheran pattern.

Square knots (see Macramé chapter 2, page 154) are a simple but effective technique. Worked in a series, they make useful braid which can take on entirely different looks depending on the yarn. For example, crochet cotton would make a braid fine enough for a child's dress, while a thick wool braid would be useful for decorating an upholstered chair or a tweed jacket.

But varying the yarn is not the only way to give interest to square knot braid. It is also possible to add picots, side knots, beads or rings.

Square knots with picots
Set on 2 doubled threads and make one square knot. Work a second square knot leaving a space between it and the first one. Push the knot up into place under the first one. The length of thread left between the two knots dictates the size of the picot.

Square knots with side knots
Set on doubled threads and work a square knot. Tie an overhand knot on each of the right and left threads, using a pin to slide the knots up against the preceding square knot before finally tightening it. Make a second square knot.

Square knots with beads
Set on 2 doubled threads and make one square knot. Thread a bead onto each of the left- and right-hand threads and work a second square knot.
N.B. Choose beads which have large holes so they are easily threaded. Children's china or wooden threading beads, and small rings available for various purposes from notions departments, all add an attractive three-dimensional look to macramé.

Lampshade

You will need
- [ ] 2 balls Polypropylene string
- [ ] One 5in lampshade ring with light fitting
- [ ] One 6in ring
- [ ] One 7in ring
(If you can't find lampshade fittings use embroidery hoops.)
- [ ] 32½ in diameter rings

Size
7in wide at widest part
10in deep including fringe

To make a lampshade
Cut 38 threads each 80 inches long. Set on 19 sets of 2 doubled threads, each with 2 picots and one square knot before being knotted onto first 5 inch ring. Work one round of square knots. Slot the left-hand thread of each knot and the right-hand thread of the knot immediately to the left through the same ring all the way around and then work another row of square knots. Work one row of alternate square knots. Using a separate thread, work one row half hitches, darning in ends afterward. Using the same grouping in fours as on previous row of square knots, work 8 square knots on each group.

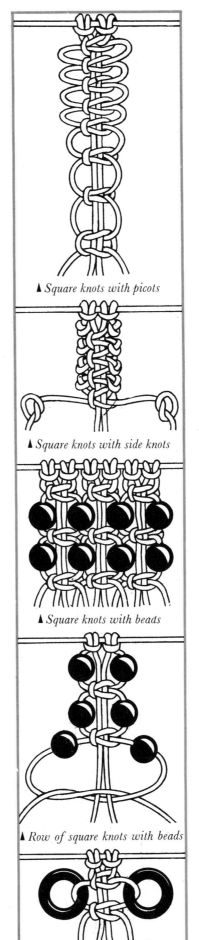

▲ *Square knots with picots*

▲ *Square knots with side knots*

▲ *Square knots with beads*

▲ *Row of square knots with beads*

▲ *Square knots with rings*

Work one row half hitches onto 7 inch ring. Divide the threads into alternate groups of four and work a further 8 square knots. Work a row of half hitches over the 6 inch ring. Work one row square knots, link groups with rings as before and work a further row of square knots. Work one row alternate square knots. Using separate length of thread, work 2 rows half hitches. Darn in the ends of the separate thread and even up remaining thread to make fringe. Fray out.

Teheran pattern

This attractive pattern, although open enough to require backing, is smooth enough to

be useful for pillows or chair seat covers.

Set on 2 white doubled threads, 1 light blue, 2 dark blue, 1 light blue, 2 white. This makes one motif—work in multiples of these 16 threads. Work 2 rows half hitches.

Working from left to right, make one half hitch on the first left-hand thread with the second, and another on the third with the fourth. Using these 4 white threads as a base, work diagonal half hitches from right to left with 2 light and 2 dark blue threads. Work in the same way but in the opposite direction for the right half of the motif. The white threads are now grouped in the center of the motif.

To work the central white diamond, half hitch the second thread from the left over the first, then fourth over third. Using the next two threads together as one leader, half hitch diagonally to the left. Next, half hitch the fourth thread over third, and sixth over fifth, and half hitch to left using seventh and eighth threads together as one leader. Finally, half hitch the sixth over the fifth, and eighth over seventh. This completes white diamond. Work all the way along the width of the fabric down to this level, making eight-thread square knots between the diamonds, working with the dark blue threads over a core of light blue threads. At each end where there are groups of 4 threads, half hitch the outer 2 over the inner 2. Next half hitch over the groups of four white threads to left and right as they lie. On the next row, half hitch the left-hand group of white threads second over first, and fourth over third. Make a square knot with light blue threads over a cord of dark blue, make diamonds with the white threads as before and at the right-hand edge half hitch the outside white thread over the one before and third over fourth thread in.

Repeat from the beginning as required.

Pillow

You will need
- [ ] 2 50grm balls knitting worsted in each of white, light blue and dark blue
- [ ] ½yd toning cotton material
- [ ] Pillow form 16in by 12in

Size
16in by 12in

To make the pillow
Work from the long side. Set threads in groups of 16 and work about 12 inches. Finish with one row horizontal half hitches, sew in ends. Make the pillow cover in toning fabric, then stitch the macramé on one side. Work a square knot braid in dark blue about 56 inches long to trim edges.

▲ *An attractive lampshade decorated with rings*

▼ *Teheran pattern for a hardwearing pillow*

Making a soft-tailored coat

In this chapter Creative Hands introduces you to soft tailoring with a simple, fitted coat. The pattern is from Vogue and matches the dress in the previous chapter.

The instructions supplied with the pattern have been specially developed in the following pages to help you gain a feeling for making larger and heavier garments without the intricacies involved in real tailoring.

The coat is made in a synthetic knit. Man-made knits make soft tailoring easy as the fabric itself is soft and pliable, but firm, and the instructions given here are specially geared to its use. Other types of fabrics often demand real tailoring techniques which require specialized knowledge.

The coat

Suitable fabrics
Polyester knit is a good choice as it will help to retain the shape of the fairly full skirted coat.
Acrylics such as Acrilan are also suitable, provided they do not drop heavily.

Interfacing, lining, trimmings
The interfacing used for the coat made in a synthetic fiber fabric is Pellon which can be of the iron-on type if you feel confident enough to use it. If not, use an appropriate weight of ordinary Pellon. Most stores selling Pellon have the manufacturer's guide to its usage and will be able to advise you on the correct type for your fabric.

For the coat lining choose a light-weight synthetic taffeta which is soft and easy to work. These qualities are essential when lining knit garments with set-in sleeves. Stiff linings form points especially at the fullness of the lining sleeve crown which would affect the smooth finish of the set-in sleeves.

Buttons and trimmings should have smooth edges so that they cannot catch in the stitches of the knit.
Other accessories needed are given on the pattern envelope.

The pattern pieces
For the coat you will need pattern pieces 10, 12, 13, 14, 15, 16, 17, 18, 20, 21 and 23.
You will also need the pattern pieces for the lining, numbers 22, 24, 25, 26, 27 and 28.

The pattern size
A coat or jacket pattern has much more ease built into it than a dress pattern. This means the finished garment can be worn over dresses and other garments without fitting too tightly. The armholes too are slightly larger to fit around other sleeves without straining.

The amount of built-in ease is usually 4 to 5 inches more than the body measurements depending on the style of the garment. The ease can be as much as 10 inches when a garment is designed with a particularly heavy fabric in mind.

Make sure that you choose your size according to the measurements given on the pattern envelope, and when adjusting the pattern, only take out of the pattern width the difference between your own measurement and that stated on the pattern envelope. Any further adjustments should be made when fitting the garment.

Adjusting the pattern
As with dressmaking, in soft tailoring all finer interfacings can be taken into the seams when stitching without adding too much bulk. So to cut out the interfacing use the front facings (14 and 23), sleeve facing (18) and under collar (13) pattern pieces.
Pin the front facing pattern pieces to the front edges of the bodice and skirt as for the robe in Dressmaking chapter 39, page 774, figure 1. This will eliminate bulky seams along the front edges.

Cutting out
Adjust the layout on the instruction sheet to suit the adapted pattern pieces.
With coats always cut 1 inch seam allowances since the fabric may need a little more ease than allowed for.
Make sure that the fabric layers are smooth before pinning on the pattern.
Working on a longer length of fabric which is also weightier than you are used to, you may find a little distortion in the finish of the cloth when you try to make the selvages meet. In short lengths this can be easily stroked out and the fabric allowed to go the way it will, but in longer lengths this may prove to be an irritation because of the drag of the fabric.
So, first lay the full length of the fabric on a flat surface and make the selvages meet having allowed the fabric to fall as it will. Pin the selvages together. Do not try and force the fabric as this would result in the fold line twisting and you would cut an unevenly fitting garment.

Marking the pattern details
You are working on larger areas which require more handling than dress sections, so mark the pattern details with care.
Any markings which have to last until the end of the work, such as hemlines or waistlines, must be marked again with a long row of basting stitches after the layers are separated.

▼ *Vogue Pattern. Dress front with shaped bodice seam: coat back*

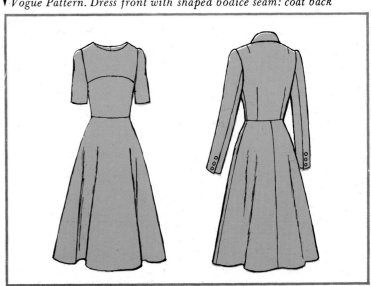

Fitting

Following the pattern instructions, pin and baste the coat together for fitting.

Fit the coat over clothing similar to that which you intend to wear under it. The coat should fit softly to the contours of the body but not too closely, even at the waist. Make the coat waistline ½ inch longer than your natural waistline.

The sleeve line of a coat falls well outside that of a dress. The crown of each sleeve should roll gently over the outside shoulder edge but not fall over it.

The front line of the armhole must follow in a good line from the shoulder into the underarm, where it must deepen a little. Test the width across the back by stretching your arms forward to make sure you have enough room for movement.

Making the coat

When making tailored garments, complete as much work as possible on each section before joining them. This way you avoid a heavy weight dragging in your hands as you complete the finer hand work. In addition, you can press and keep smooth those sections which would be inaccessible to thorough pressing when the garment is completed.

Leave the work spread out on a surface to support the weight whenever possible. Tailors used to sit cross-legged on a table for this very reason.

Mark out all the fitting details then rip all the sections.

Make the coat bodice first.

Working on the Back, stitch and press the darts, then pin the Back to a stand.

Pin the front interfacing to the wrong side of each Front, with the seamline of the interfacing coinciding with the fold line of the Front wrap edge.

Work a row of prick stitches to secure the interfacing to the fold line and attach the inside edge to the coat fabric with long herringbone stitches, leaving enough space at the shoulders and waist to sew the sections together.

Stitch and press the Front darts. Make bound buttonholes as shown opposite.

Stitch and press the shoulder and side seams.

Lap the interfacing over the shoulder seams and finish sewing the inside edge to the coat fabric.

Prepare the under collar as shown in steps 7 to 10 on the instruction sheet.

To give the under collar extra support and assist the Center Back roll, stitch to each side of the seam through all layers of fabric as shown (figure **1**).

Stitch on the under collar as shown in step 11.

Stitch the facings as in step 12, remember-
1258

ing that the front facings have been cut onto the Front.

Attach the upper collar as shown in step 15. If you are working with a knit fabric the upper collar will not need an underlining (see step 14).

When a separate pattern is supplied for upper and under collar a certain amount of ease is built into the upper collar pattern. However, this ease may not be right for all types of fabrics, and may even disappear as you pin the upper collar to the under collar.

If you find that this has happened to your collar, ease a little of the seam allowance

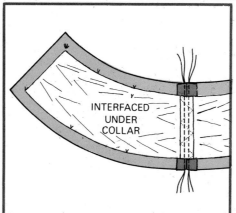

INTERFACED UNDER COLLAR

▲ **1.** *Under collar seam stitched to each side*
into the upper collar. This is necessary to keep the seam edges from showing after the collar has been turned and finished.

Stitch the collar sections together (step 16) and then stitch the top edge of the wrap.

Turn the collar to the right side and the facing inside (step 17). Edge-baste the collar and press. Do any pressing gently as hard pressing would cause the seam edges to make an impression on the outside fabric. So work over the collar several times with light strokes and movements.

While the collar is still warm curve it in your hand. This will help it to roll beautifully.

Work step 18.

Make the sleeves as shown in steps 19 to 25. Also line the sleeves at this stage (see steps 14 to 17, and 20 under Lining section), but do not catch the lining in with the sleeve seam. Insert the sleeves following steps 26 and 27.

Make the skirt following steps 28 to 32 and pin and baste the hem lightly.

Press the large areas of the skirt as for the final pressing and leave them to cool before attaching skirt to bodice. Stitch the bodice to the skirt working steps 33 and 34.

Try on the coat to check the length, then finish the hem, steps 37 and 38.

Make the lining as shown under Lining, steps 1 to 9.

To avoid distortion in the lining, slip the coat over a dress form, wrong side out, then slip over the lining, right side out.

Following steps 10 to 13 attach the lining to the coat with invisible slip stitches and secure it to the armhole seam allowances with small basting stitches.

Fold in the seam allowances of the lining sleeve cap and sew to the armhole seamline with firm felling stitches.

Work steps 35 and 36 and give the edge of the coat a final pressing.

Using double buttonhole twist, crochet a coat hanger 3 inches long. Press it flat and attach it to the wrong side of the coat across the Center Back neck edge along the seamline. Stitch through several layers of fabric to anchor it firmly.

Finish the waistline with a self-made, or ready-made, belt.

Bound Buttonholes

There is one basic technique for making bound buttonholes which is varied according to the type of fabric used.

The fabric

The fabric on which the bound buttonholes are being made must have some depth into which the extra fabric used for binding the buttonhole can sink, otherwise the binding will create bulk and rise above the fabric surface.

Fabrics which fray easily must be prevented from fraying first. This is achieved by lining the binding for the buttonhole as well as the area for the buttonhole itself. Fabrics which fray even after these precautions are unsuitable.

The size

When using thick coating fabric make sure the buttonhole is not less than ¾ inch long. If shorter, there will not be enough length to work it properly and the buttonhole will look lumpy.

Unlike hand-worked buttonholes which have a solidly stitched edge, bound buttonholes are soft and give a little, so it is not necessary to make an extra allowance when measuring out the length of the buttonhole—the buttonhole can be made to the exact diameter of the button. However, if the button is exceptionally thick add half the thickness of the button to the length for ease.

Stitch size

The stitching needs to be very firm and small as it comes very close to the buttonhole opening.

Engage the smallest stitch setting on your machine and stitch two layers of fabric together. The stitches should be about the size of a pinpoint.

Width

The buttonhole width depends upon the type of fabric you are working on. If made in thick fabrics the buttonholes should be about $\frac{3}{8}$ inch wide, but in thin fabrics you can make them quite narrow—about $\frac{3}{16}$ to $\frac{1}{4}$ inch wide.

Making the buttonholes

Here are step by step instructions:

☐ Measure out the buttonhole positions and length, and mark them as shown (figure **2**).

☐ For each buttonhole cut a strip of fabric on the bias 2 inches wide and $1\frac{1}{2}$ inches longer than the buttonhole length. Working on the outside of the garment, lay the strip over the center of the buttonhole position with right sides of the fabric facing (figure **3**).

☐ Working on the wrong side of the fabric, stitch the outline of the buttonhole, shaping it into a perfect rectangle and carefully pivoting the work on the needle at each corner (figure **4**). Run the last stitches over the first stitches as shown, to prevent the buttonhole from splitting.

☐ Using sharp, pointed scissors, cut into the stitched area as shown (figure **5**) being careful not to cut the stitches at the corners.

☐ Pull the binding fabric to the inside (figure **6**). Then lay each buttonhole seam allowance over the edge of a sleeveboard and press the seam allowances away from the opening as shown.

☐ **Small buttonholes.** For small buttonholes, turn the work to the outside and gently roll the folded edges of the binding so that they meet along the center of the buttonhole with equal width to each side (figure **7**). Lightly baste along the opening as shown.

Turn the work to the inside and gently pull the horizontal edges of the binding fabric to make the rolls continue evenly beyond the opening of the buttonhole. Catch them together permanently with matching thread (figure **8**).

☐ **Large buttonholes.** Large buttonholes are made as above but each rolled edge must be worked separately. As it is rolled it must be secured with small prick stitches along the fold of the seamline on the right side (figure **9**). Do not pull the stitches tight into the fabric or they will make dents which will show in the finished work.

Baste along the opening (figure **10**) then stitch the ends of the rolled edges together on the wrong side as shown in figure **8**.

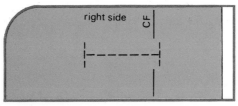

▲ **2.** *The marked out buttonhole*

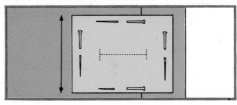

▲ **3.** *The bias strip laid over the buttonhole*

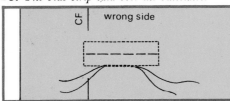

▲ **4.** *The stitched rectangle for the buttonhole*

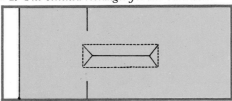

▲ **5.** *Cutting the buttonhole*

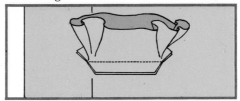

▲ **6.** *The binding pulled through the opening*

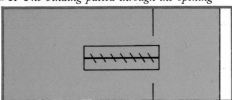

▲ **7.** *The rolled edges on a small buttonhole*

☐ With the basting stitches still in place, carefully press each buttonhole. Then, while the work is still warm from the iron, gently pull the ends of the rolled edges of the bias strip to settle them into the fabric and fix the shape of the buttonhole. Remove any impressions made in the fabric by pressing under the binding fabric strip.

Turn the garment facing over the buttonholes and baste the front edge of the facing firmly in position.

Feel the buttonhole through the facing fabric and make a cut through the facing to the length of the buttonhole opening. Turn in the edges of the cut and hem them

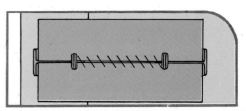

▲ **8.** *The rolled edges sewn at the sides*

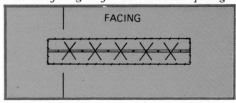

▲ **9.** *Large buttonhole: the prick-stitched edge*

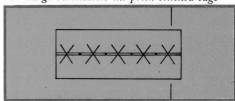

▲ **10.** *The basted opening of a large buttonhole*

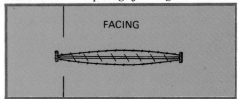

▲ **11.** *The facing cut for the buttonhole opening*

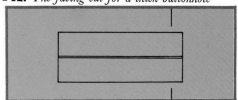

▲ **12.** *The facing cut for a thick buttonhole*

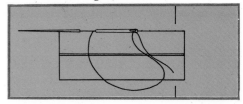

▲ **13.** *The finished buttonhole*

to the buttonhole (figure **11**).

If the ends of the cut are tight you must make the snip a little longer to take away the strain.

Make a small bar across each end as shown, to strengthen the opening.

On heavy fabric it may be necessary to cut the facing as for the buttonhole since the turning of the raw edges makes it necessary to make a cut very much longer than the opening of the buttonhole (figure **12**).

☐ Lightly press over the hemmed edges, remove the basting thread from the rolled edges of the buttonhole and give a final pressing (figure **13**).

Fashion Flair
Collars & necklines

The moods of fashion are constantly changing and collars and necklines are no exception. Collars can be big or small, plain or decorative, matching or contrasting: necklines can be scooped, square, gathered, frilled or fancy — the variations are endless. There are many beautiful trimmings available which, when used with a little imagination and know-how, can instantly make a plain garment look different and exciting.

Some variations are sketched here to give a few ideas for the perfect neckline to set off a new dress, or to transform a favorite older one.

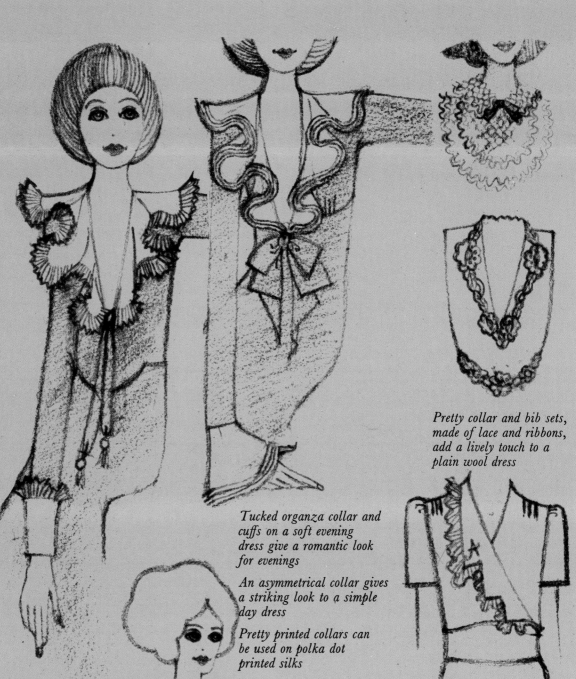

Pretty collar and bib sets, made of lace and ribbons, add a lively touch to a plain wool dress

Tucked organza collar and cuffs on a soft evening dress give a romantic look for evenings

An asymmetrical collar gives a striking look to a simple day dress

Pretty printed collars can be used on polka dot printed silks

Flowers and lace motifs give a charming finish to collars and necklines

A frilled collar and cuff set can dress up a long, plain crepe dress

A beaded collar adds a touch of luxury to a simple tunic

Pattern Library

Garden flowers

Simple flower shapes make pretty appliqué motifs for household linen. The flower sprays shown here are of fine lawn in bright, clear colors, applied to a plain cotton background. The details on leaves and petals are worked in outline stitch and backstitch. The flower centers are decorated with French knots and tiny spots of satin stitch.

Use these pretty flower sprays to decorate sheets and pillow cases, guest towels or fine table linen.

Alpine flowers on a knitted dress

Embroider sprays of flowers on this knitted dress.

When knitting is used as a base for embroidery, the usual methods of transferring embroidery designs to fabric cannot be applied and it becomes necessary to use an alternative method.

Trace the design onto tissue or tracing paper and baste the actual tracing securely onto the garment. Embroider over the paper, cutting away the surplus paper as the design is worked. The paper under the embroidery can later be eased out with a sharp needle or pin between the stitches.

Dress

Size

Directions are for 24in chest. The figures in brackets [ ] refer to the 26 and 28in sizes respectively.
Length to shoulder 23[25¼: 27½]in adjustable.

> **Gauge**
> 6 sts and 8 rows to 1in over st st worked on No.4 needles.

Materials

Sports yarn
4[5:5:6] 2oz skeins main color A
1 skein contrast B
One pair No. 3 needles (or Canadian No. 10)
One pair No. 4 needles (or Canadian No. 9)
Embroidery thread as desired
One No.F (4.00 mm) crochet hook
Tracing or tissue paper
Stitch holder

Back

**Using No.3 needles and B, cast on 148[160:172] sts.
K 8 rows.
Change to No.4 needles and A. Continue in st st beg with a K row until work measures 12[13½:15]in or 1in less than desired length to waist, ending with a K row.
Next row *P2 tog, rep from * to end of row.** 74[80:86] sts.
Work 2in in K1, P1 rib.
Continue in st st beg with a K row and inc one st at each end of 5th and following 12th row. 78[84:90] sts.
Work without shaping until work measures 3½[4:4½]in from top of ribbing, ending with a P row.

Shape armholes

Bind off 4[5:6] sts at beg of next 2 rows.
Bind off 3 sts at beg of next 2 rows.
Bind off 2 sts at beg of next 2 rows.
Bind off 1 st at beg of next 2 rows.
Work without shaping until armholes measure 3¾[4:4¼]in, ending with a P row.

Shape neck

1st row K23[24:25] sts, bind off 12[14:16] sts, K to end. Work on this group of sts for left shoulder.
Bind off at neck edge 2 sts every other row 3 times, and dec 1 st every other row 6 times.
Work without shaping until armhole measure 5½[5¾:6]in, ending the knitting at the armhole edge.

Shape shoulder

Bind off 3[4:5] sts at beg of next row. Work 1 row.
Bind off 4 sts at beg of next row. Work 1 row.
Bind off rem 4 sts.
With WS facing, attach yarn to rem sts for right shoulder. Work to correspond to left shoulder.

Front

Work from ** to ** as given for Back.
Work 1in in K1, P1 rib.

Divide for Front opening

1st row Rib 32[35:38] sts, bind off 10 sts, rib to end. Complete Right Front on these sts.
Work until 2in in K1, P1 rib is complete.
Continue in st st beg with a K row and inc one st at side edge on 5th and following 12th row. 34[37:40] sts.
Work without shaping until same length as Back to armhole, ending at side edge.

Shape armhole

Bind off 4[5:6] sts at beg of next row. Work 1 row.
Bind off 3 sts at beg of next row. Work 1 row.
Bind off 2 sts at beg of next row. Work 1 row.
Bind off 1 st at beg of next row.
Work without shaping until armhole measures 1½[1¾:2]in from beg, ending at front edge.

Shape neck

Bind off 10 sts at beg of next row. Dec one st at neck edge on next 3[4:5] rows.
Work without shaping until armhole measures same as Back to shoulder, ending at armhole edge.

Shape shoulder

Work as given for Back. With WS facing, attach yarn to rem sts for left Front and work to correspond.

Neck and Front edging

Using No.3 needles and B, with RS facing pick up and K27[30:33] sts up right Front opening from bound-off center sts to neck edge, pick up and K13[14:15] sts from bound-off center Front edge and pick up and K23[24:25] sts from side of shoulder.
1st row K22[23:24], K2 tog, K12[13:14], K up thread before next st, K27[30:33]. K 1 row.
3rd row K21[22:23], K2 tog, K12[13:14], K up thread before next st, K to end. K 1 row.
5th row K20[21:22], K2 tog, K12[13:14], K up thread

Embroider flower sprays in bright-colored yarn for an apron effect

before next st, K to end.
K 1 row.
7th row K19[20:21], K2 tog,
K12[13:14], K up thread
before next st, K to end.
K 1 row.
8th row K. Bind off.
Work other Front to match.

Back neck edging
Using No.3 needles and B,
with RS facing pick up and
K40[42:44] sts. K 8 rows.
Bind off.
Join shoulder seams. Press
lightly under damp cloth with
warm iron, omitting garter st.

Armbands
Using No.3 needles and B,
with RS facing pick up and
K64[68:72] sts evenly around
armhole. K 8 rows. Bind off.

Finishing

Join side seams.
Join edges of Front bands to
bound-off center sts.
Using A, crochet lacing and
thread through Fronts.
Make tassels of B and attach
to each end of lacing.
Trace the pattern onto paper
and baste securely in place.
Embroider as shown in
illustration. Remove paper
and ease out pieces of paper
under embroidery. Press again
lightly.

▼ *Open-petaled flower motifs*

Knitted knight's tunic

The knights of old wore a tunic for extra warmth without bulk, for color, and to keep their chain mail dry! Without the problem of rusting chain mail, tunics are still the ideal garment to wear for an extra layer of warmth with maximum freedom of movement. The front opening on this tunic fastens with frog closings.

Sizes
Directions are for 34in bust. The figures in brackets [ ] refer to the 36, 38, 40in sizes respectively.
Length at center back, 31[32:33:34]in.

Gauge
6 sts and 8 rows to 1in over pattern worked on No.5 needles.

Materials
Sports yarn
5[6:6:6] 2oz skeins
One pair No.5 needles
(or Canadian No.8)
4 frog closings

Back

Using No.5 needles, cast on 90[96:102:108] sts.
Beg with a K row work in st st.
Work 1 row.
Inc one st at each end of every row until there are 100[106:112:118] sts.
Commence patt.
1st-6th rows K.
7th row K.
8th row P.
Rep last 2 rows twice more. These 12 rows form patt and are rep throughout.
1264

Continue in patt until work measures 24[25:25½:26½]in from beg, ending with a WS row.

Shape armholes
Bind off 6 sts at beg of next 2 rows.
Dec one st at each end of every row until 80[84:88:92] sts rem.
Continue without shaping until armholes measure 7[7:7½:7½]in ending with a WS row.

Shape shoulders
Bind off 9 sts at beg of next 4 rows.
Bind off 8[9:10:11] sts at beg of next 2 rows.

Bind off rem sts.

Left front

Using No.5 needles, cast on 40[43:46:49] sts.
Beg with a K row work in st st.
Work 1 row.
Inc one st at each end of every row until there are 50[53:56:59] sts.
Continue in patt as for Back until work measures same as Back to armhole, ending with a WS row.

Shape armhole
Bind off 6 sts at beg of next row.
Dec one st at armhole edge on every row 4[5:6:7] times.
Continue without shaping until armhole measures 5in from beg, ending at center front edge.

Shape neck
Bind off 7 sts at beg of next row.
Dec one st at neck edge on every row 7[8:9:10] times.
Continue without shaping until armhole measures same as Back to shoulder, ending at armhole edge.

Shape Shoulder
Bind off 9 sts every other row twice.
Bind off rem 8[9:10:11] sts.

Right front

Work as for Left front, ending with a RS row before armhole shaping.

Finishing

Press lightly.
Join shoulder seams using back st.

Armbands
Pick up and K95[95:101:101] sts evenly around armhole with RS facing. Beg with a P row work 5 rows st st, inc one st at each end of every row.
Bind off loosely.
Join side seams using back st and leaving 9in free at bottom of seams to form side vents.

Vents
Pick up and K54 sts evenly along one side of vent, with RS facing. Beg with a P row work 5 rows st st, dec one st at lower edge of vent and inc one st at other end of row. Bind off loosely.
Work 3 other vent edges.

Front facings
Pick up and K173[179:182: 188] sts along edge of Right front, with RS facing. Beg with a P row work 5 rows st st, dec one st at lower edge on every row. Bind off loosely.
Work left front in same way.
Fold all st st edges to WS of Tunic and slip st in place, joining mitered corners.

Collar
Pick up and K70[74:84:88] sts evenly around neck, with RS facing and beg 3 sts in from center front edges. Beg with a K row work 5 rows garter st, 4 rows st st, 6 rows garter st and 12 rows st st.
Bind off loosely.
Fold collar in half to WS and slip st in place, sewing down side edges.
Sew on closings.

The tunic with a distinctive metal clasp fastening

Tunic with link fastening ▶

Windowpane snowflakes in crochet

This charming idea for displaying fine crochet comes from Scandinavia. These delicate motifs are worked onto metal rings. To show their snowflake pattern to its best advantage, hang them singly or in groups against a windowpane.

Sizes

Large 12 leaf daisy 9½in diameter.
Large 6 pointed star 9½in diameter.
Small 12 leaf daisy 5¼in diameter.
Small 8 pointed star 5¼in diameter.
Small 6 pointed star 5¼in diameter.

Materials

For each design, Coats & Clark's O.N.T. Pearl Cotton 2 (50 yd) balls
One No.G (4.50 mm) crochet hook
Wire to bend into rings 9½ or 5¼in in diameter
NB All 5 designs can be made from 6 balls, and all the 3 small designs can be made from only 2 balls.

Large 12 leaf daisy ring

Ch10, join into a circle with a ss into first ch.
1st round Ch2, 23dc into circle. Join with a ss into 2nd of 2ch.
2nd round Ch4, 3tr in next st leaving last loop of each tr on hook, yoh and draw through all loops, (ch5, skip 1 st, 4tr in next st leaving last loop of each tr on hook, yoh and draw through all loops—called 1cl—) 11

1266

times, ch5. Join with a ss into 2nd of 2ch.
3rd round (Ch5, 1sc in top of next cl) 11 times, ch5. Join with a ss into top of 1st cl.
4th round (Ch4, 1dc in ch5 sp, ch4, 1sc in next sc) 12 times.
5th round Ss into first dc, (ch9, 1sc in next dc) 12 times.
6th round Ch4, 3tr in last sc of 5th round leaving last loop of each tr on hook, yoh, draw through all loops, (ch7, 1sc in ch9 sp, ch7, 1cl as for 2nd round in next sc) 11 times, ch7, 1sc in ch9 sp, ch7, ss into top of first cl.
7th round Ss over first ch3 of first ch7 loop, 1sc in next ch, (ch3, 1tr in next sc, ch3, 1sc in center ch of next ch7 loop, ch5, 1sc in center ch of next ch7 loop) 12 times. Join with a ss into first sc.
8th round Ss into next tr, ch6, (4dc in next ch5 sp, ch4, 1dc in tr, ch4) 11 times, 4dc in ch5 sp, ch4. Join with a ss into 2nd of 6ch.
Ring joining round 1sc over ring, (14sc over ring, 1sc in center of next 4dc gr, 14sc over ring, 1sc in next dc) rep around circle. Join with a ss into first sc. Fasten off leaving 12in length of cotton to use for hanging circle.

Small 12 leaf daisy ring

Work as for large 12 leaf daisy to end of 4th round.
Ring joining round Ss into next dc, (14sc over ring, 1sc in next dc) 11 times, 14sc over ring, ss into first sc. Fasten off as for large daisy.

Small 8 pointed star ring

Ch12. Join with a ss into first ch to form circle.
1st round Ch2, 23dc into circle. Join with a ss into 2nd of 2ch.
2nd round (Ch5, skip 2 sts, 1sc in next st, ch4, skip 2 sts, 1sc in next st) 4 times.
3rd round Ss into ch5 sp, ch2, 3dc in ch5 sp, ch3, 4dc in same sp, 1sc in ch4 sp, (work 4dc, ch3, 4dc all in next ch5 sp, 1sc in next ch4 sp) 3 times, ss into 2nd of 2ch.
4th round Ss into next ch3 sp, ch7, 1sc in same sp, (ch5, 1dc in next sc, ch5, 1sc in ch3 sp, ch7, 1sc in

same sp) 3 times, ch5, 1dc in next sc, ch5. Join with a ss into first ss.
5th round (Work 4sc, ch3, 4sc all in ch7 sp, ch4, 4dc in 1dc, ch4) 4 times. Join with a ss into first sc.
Ring joining round Ss into center of ch3 sp, 1sc over ring, (18sc over ring, 1sc in center of 4dc gr, 18sc over ring, 1sc in ch3 sp) 4 times.
Fasten off as for large daisy.

Small 6 pointed star ring

Ch12. Join with a ss into first ch to form circle.
1st round Work 18sc

into ring.

2nd round Ch3, 2dc in first st, ch5, 1sc into 4th of 5ch, ch1—called 1 picot—, skip 2 sts, (3dc in next sc, 1 picot, skip 2 sts) 5 times. Join with a ss into 3rd of 3ch.

3rd round Ch3, 1dc in first dc, 1dc in next dc, 2dc in next dc, 1 picot, (2dc in next dc, 1dc in next dc, 2dc in next dc, 1 picot) 5 times. Join with a ss into top of 3ch.

4th round Ch3, 1dc in first dc, 1dc in each of next 3dc, 2dc in next dc, 1 picot, (2dc in next dc, 1dc in each of next 3dc, 2dc in next dc, 1 picot) 5 times. Join with a ss into 3rd of 3ch.

5th round (Ch6, 1sc in

center dc of 7dc gr, ch6, 1sc in last dc of 7dc gr, ch6, 1sc in first dc of next 7dc group) rep all around circle. Join with a ss into base of first 6ch.

Ring joining round Ss into center of next ch6 sp, 1sc over ring, (7sc over ring, 1sc in next ch6 sp), rep all around circle. Join with a ss into first sc. Fasten off leaving 12in length for hanging.

Large 6 pointed star ring

Work as small 6 pointed star ring to end of 4th round.

5th round Ch3, 1dc in first dc, 1dc in each of next 5dc, 2dc in next dc, 1 picot, (2dc in

next dc, 1dc in each of next 5dc, 2dc in next dc, 1 picot) 5 times. Join with a ss into 3rd of first 3ch.

6th round Ch3, 1dc in each of 2nd, 3rd and 4th dc leaving last loop of each dc on hook, yoh and draw through all loops, ch4, skip 1dc, 1dc in each of next 4dc leaving last loop of each dc on hook, yoh and draw through all loops—called 1cl—, ch4, 3dc in picot, ch4, (1cl, ch4, skip 1dc, 1cl, ch4, 3dc in picot, ch4) 5 times. Join with a ss into top of first cl.

7th round Ss into next ch4 sp, ch3, 6dc into sp, 1 picot, 1dc in center dc of 3dc, 1 picot, (7dc in next ch4 sp, 1 picot,

1dc in center of 3dc, 1 picot) 5 times. Join with a ss into 3rd of 3ch.

8th round Ch3, 1dc in first dc, 1dc in each of next 2dc, ch3, skip 1dc, 1dc in each of next 2dc, 2dc in next dc, 1 picot, 3dc in next dc, 1 picot, (2dc in next dc, 1dc in each of next 2dc, ch3, skip 1dc, 1dc in each of next 2dc, 2dc in next dc, 1 picot, 3dc in next dc, 1 picot) 5 times. Join with a ss into 3rd of 3ch.

Ring joining round Ss into center of next ch3 sp, *(18sc over ring, 1sc in next picot) twice, 18sc over ring, 1sc in next ch3 sp, rep from * 5 times more. Fasten off, leaving 12in length for hanging.

Fresh as a daisy

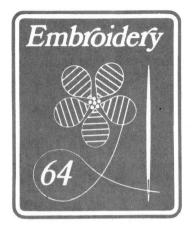

White marguerite daisies embroidered in padded satin stitch make a fresh and pleasing design for an elegant circular tablecloth and a set of matching napkins.

Buy a circular tablecloth and a set of napkins, or to make a circular tablecloth measuring 72 inches in diameter, and six napkins measuring 16 inches square, you will need:
- ☐ 3¼yds 80 inch wide cotton and Dacron
- ☐ 4½yds bias binding to match tablecloth fabric
- ☐ D.M.C. 6-strand floss in the following colors: 8 skeins white, 4 skeins cream 712, 4 skeins bright green 906, 4 skeins dark green 895.
- ☐ Crewel needle No. 8
- ☐ White carbon paper

Transferring the design
Divide the cloth into four sections with lines of basting stitches. Trace the flower motifs and using white carbon paper transfer them to the cloth in a centered circular arrangement. Transfer the single daisy motif onto each of the napkins.

Stitches
The flower petals and leaves are worked in padded satin stitch using three strands of floss in the needle. The stems are worked in outline stitch with three strands in the needle and the flower centers are a mass of French knots using four strands of floss.

▲ *The five-petaled daisy motif with its clustered French knots*

▼ *Arrange eight of the five-petaled daisies for the circular design*

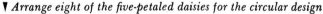

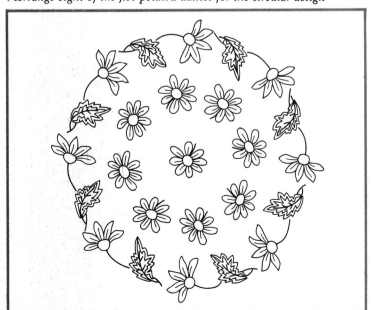

▲ *The eight-petaled daisies are grouped in the middle of the cloth*   ▼ *Daisy patterns. Use the three-petaled flower for napkins*

Slip covers the easy way

Here are the step by step instructions for making slip covers for square back armchairs with box cushions—a note about covering round back chairs is included. Whatever the shape you are covering, you will find that the same principles apply.

Suitable fabrics

Choose a good fabric like linen or sturdy cotton, one that is strong and evenly woven and will neither stretch nor shrink.

Patterns

It is possible to buy paper patterns for different shapes of chair, but it is often more successful to make your own cover with measurements from the chair, and then fit and refit it until it is absolutely correct.

Measuring

If the fabric you choose has a pattern, allow extra yardage for a pattern repeat (usually about one yard extra for matching and placing the pattern). An easy guide, though not reliable without checking, is that you will need about five times the height of the back of the chair in fabric.

Normally, if the armchair is fairly large, most of the width of the fabric will be used, but keep the remnants for front facings, bindings, piping and base pieces.

Should you want pleats or a flounce around the lower edge of the cover, which will make the cover correspondingly shorter, you will need to estimate the amount of extra fabric needed for this. Also allow extra piping between cover and

Home Sewing 19

flounce (see notes on measuring for piping below).
Instructions for measuring and making pleats and flounces appear in Home Sewing 4, p. 392. Parts of the chair and seams to be piped are shown in figure 1. Piping is shown in red.

How to measure

Use a firm linen or plastic tape measure and measure the following:
Figure 2. i. The outside back from A1 to the floor or to the length required. Add 2 inches for seams.
  ii. The top edge from A1 to A2. Add 2 inches for seams.
  iii. The side edge from K1 to K2. Add 2 inches for seams.
  iv. The side edge from S to T. Add 2 inches for seams.
  v. The outside back from K1 to L1. Add 2 inches for seams.
Figure 3. vi. The inside back from A2 to B. Add 10 inches for seams and tuck in.
  vii. The seat from B to C. Add 8 inches for seams and tuck in.
  viii. The front from C to D. Add 2 inches for seams.
  ix. The outside arm from G to H. Add 2 inches for seams.
  x. The inside arm from G to J. Add 8 inches for seams and tuck in.
Figure 4. xi. The inside back from L2 to K2. Add 2 inches for seams.
  xii. The seat from E to F. Add 10 inches for tuck in and seams.

  xiii. The front from M to N. Add 2 inches for seams.
  xiv. The front facing from U to V. Add 2 inches for seams.
  xv. The front facing from W to X. Add 2 inches for seams.
  xvi. The outside arm from Q to R. Add 2 inches for seams.
  xvii. The inside arm from O to P. Add 5 inches for seams and tuck in.
Add together measurements i, ii, vi, vii, viii, ix and x. The total will give you the amount of fabric needed. This does not allow for pattern matching.
Piping. When measuring is completed, measure all the seams that will need to be piped (see figure 1), on average about 10 yards.
You will need piping cord to the same measurement and make sure that this is pre-shrunk. If you are not sure, buy an extra yard of cord, boil the cord in water and leave it to dry overnight.
It is estimated that $\frac{1}{2}$yd 48in wide fabric will make about 10 yards of bias strip. Try to use up all the remnants that are left over after cutting.

Cutting out

Here are some general notes on cutting before you start on each piece.
Make sure that the lengthwise measurement for each piece runs with the grain of the fabric, and if it has a pattern make sure that this pattern is centered. It will help to throw each section of fabric over the chair before cutting it to see that the pattern will look right.
As you cut out each fabric piece, identify it in some way; either by labeling it with paper and a pin, or by basting on the number of each piece in a brightly colored thread.
Always be generous when you cut the fabric, it is easy to cut away more, but very difficult to add to a tight fit. Remember also that you may have to cope with shrinkage when you wash the cover, and unless the fabric is pre-shrunk,

you will have to allow for shrinkage in the seam allowances.
Mark a line down the center of all the pieces with chalk or basting thread on the true grain of the fabric. This is a safe guide to show you that the pieces do not get pulled out of shape during fitting.
Mark the inside back center of the chair with pins or chalk.
Cut the fabric as you need it. Always place the fabric pieces on the chair with the right side to the chair and the wrong side of the fabric facing you.
Seam allowance is always 1 inch.

Piece 1. The inside back. Cut a length from the fabric equal to the measurement vi. Cut the width to measurement xi.
Match the center line marked on the fabric to the center line on the chair back so that there is a good 1 inch seam allowance at the top (the highest point of the chair).
Smooth piece 1 down. Draw a curved line from point Z to the center line (figure 5). Point Z can be found by pushing your hand down the tuck in at the junction of the arm, seat and back and feeling, from the construction of the chair, what tuck in allowance should be made there.
Cut off the piece below line Z to B. Do the same for the tuck in at the junction of the arm and back, which must be shaped from * tapering just to seam allowance at the top of the arm (point Y). Mark this and cut it out (figure 6).
Take piece 1 off the chair and fold it in half down the center line and shape the other half to correspond. Put piece 1 back onto the chair.
Piece 2. The seat. Cut a length from the fabric equal to measurement vii. Cut the width to measurement xii. Place this piece on the chair seat and shape the tuck in at the back where it will join the arm. Point * on figures 5 and 6 is the meeting point for all the tuck in seams.
Push the tuck ins for pieces 1 and 2 down into the chair.

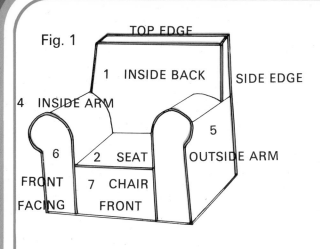

Fig. 1

TOP EDGE

1 INSIDE BACK

SIDE EDGE

4 INSIDE ARM

5

6

2 SEAT OUTSIDE ARM

FRONT

7 CHAIR

FACING CHAIR FRONT

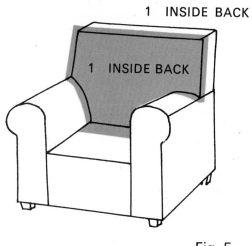

1 INSIDE BACK

1 INSIDE BACK

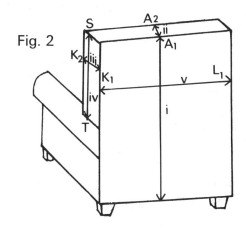

Fig. 2

S A₂ ii

A₁

K₂ iii

K₁ L₁

iv v

i

T

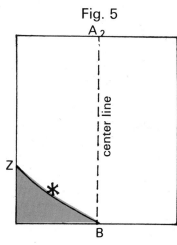

Fig. 5

A₂

center line

Z

*

B

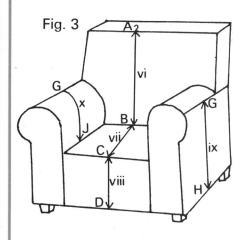

Fig. 3

A₂

vi

G

x

J B

vii

C

viii

D

G

ix

H

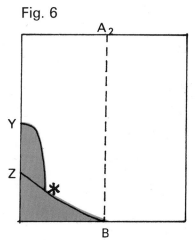

Fig. 6

A₂

Y

Z

*

B

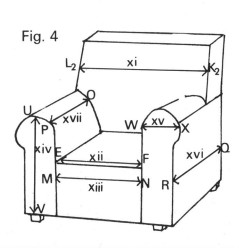

Fig. 4

L₂ xi K₂

O

U xvii

P W xv X

xiv E

xii F xvi Q

M N R

xiii

V

2 THE SEAT

1 INSIDE BACK

*

2 SEAT

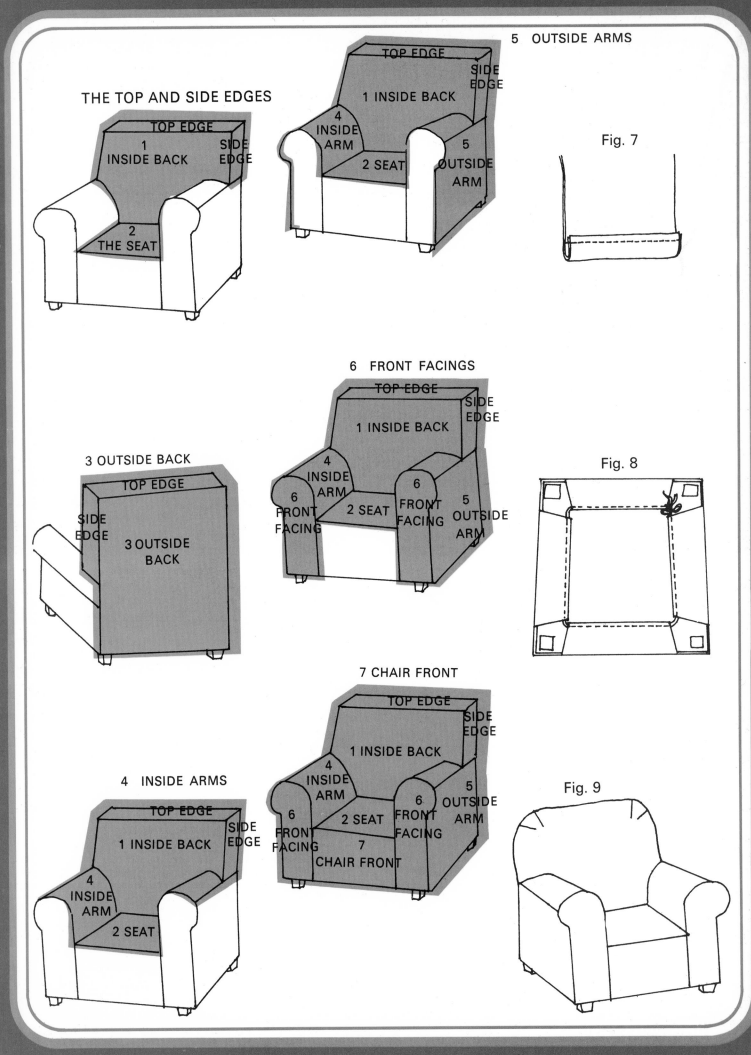

5 OUTSIDE ARMS

THE TOP AND SIDE EDGES

TOP EDGE

1 INSIDE BACK

SIDE EDGE

2 THE SEAT

TOP EDGE

SIDE EDGE

1 INSIDE BACK

4 INSIDE ARM

2 SEAT

5 OUTSIDE ARM

Fig. 7

6 FRONT FACINGS

TOP EDGE

SIDE EDGE

1 INSIDE BACK

4 INSIDE ARM

6 FRONT FACING

2 SEAT

6 FRONT FACING

5 OUTSIDE ARM

Fig. 8

3 OUTSIDE BACK

TOP EDGE

SIDE EDGE

3 OUTSIDE BACK

7 CHAIR FRONT

TOP EDGE

SIDE EDGE

1 INSIDE BACK

4 INSIDE ARM

6 FRONT FACING

2 SEAT

6 FRONT FACING

5 OUTSIDE ARM

7 CHAIR FRONT

Fig. 9

4 INSIDE ARMS

TOP EDGE

SIDE EDGE

1 INSIDE BACK

4 INSIDE ARM

2 SEAT

The top edge. Cut a piece across the fabric equal in length to measurement v, and in width to measurement ii. Match and pin this to the top edge of piece 1.

The side edges. Cut 2 pieces across the fabric each equal in length to measurement iv, and in width to measurement iii. Match and pin these to the side edges of piece 1 and to the sides of the top edge piece.

Piece 3. The outside back. Cut a length from the fabric equal to measurement i. Cut the width to measurement v. Match and pin the top center of this to the center of the top edge piece. Pin the sides of this piece to the side edges.

Pieces 4. The inside arms. Cut 2 lengths from the fabric each equal to measurement x. Cut the width of each piece to measurement xvii.

Place each piece on its respective arm and shape the tuck in to correspond with the back and seat tuck in.

Where the arm section meets the back, the tuck in will again taper to seam allowance at the top as shown for piece 1, and the seam allowance here will need to be clipped to take the curve.

Pin a piece 4 to piece 1 at the junction of the arm and back and push all the tuck ins down the chair until fitting is completed. Repeat this with the other piece 4.

Pieces 5. The outside arms. Cut 2 lengths of fabric each equal to measurement ix. Cut the width of each piece to measurement xvi. Place pieces 5 on their respective arms, matching the top of each piece to the top of each piece 4. Make sure that the crosswise thread of the fabric is parallel to the ground.

Pin the pieces 5 to pieces 4, and to the base of the side edge pieces and to the sides of piece 3.

Pieces 6. The front facings. These are cut from the remnants after cutting pieces 5. They should be as long as measurement xiv and as wide as measurement xv. Pin the pieces 6 to the front of each

arm, shaping the edges as you pin them to pieces 4 and 5.

Piece 7. The chair front. Cut a length from the fabric equal to measurement viii and as wide as measurement xiii. Pin this piece to pieces 2 and 6.

Fitting and pinning

Go over the entire cover again, repinning and readjusting the shape so that it fits perfectly. Check that the center lines marked on each piece are straight. Pay particular attention to the front facings (pieces 6) as these will attract the most attention. Check that all the seam allowances are trimmed to 1 inch.

Take care and time over adjusting the pins, making sure that the seams are pinned at regular intervals and that the pins are quite close together and pushed in properly so that they will not fall out. You may then find that basting is unnecessary and the pins can easily be removed during machining. If you wish to baste, do so now, along the pin lines. Nothing has been stitched yet.

Piping

Cover the required amount of piping cord with bias cut fabric (instructions for this are given in Home Sewing 2, p. 288, and 11, p. 872). The covered piping should have ½ inch seam allowance.

Stretch the finished piping by pulling it and do not worry if the thread snaps in places.

Pin the piping between the pieces along the back seams. Clip the seam allowance of the piping on the curves and do not pull the piping too tight. To pin in the piping, remove a few pins at a time, insert the piping and then repin.

Insert piping around the front facings, and all other piped seams shown in figure **1**.

Open one of the back seams at the lower edge as far as is necessary to allow you to ease the pinned cover off the chair. The piping should be pinned to one side of this opening only. Turn under and hem the raw edge on the other side of this opening to finish it.

Stitching

Using a zipper foot on the sewing machine, stitch all the seams close to the piping. Tuck in seams should be placed together with the raw edges matching, folded over together once and stitched through all four thicknesses (figure **7**).

Stitch the piping onto one side of the back opening only and stitch in zipper, snap fastener tape or touch and close fastening to close the opening.

Turn the cover to the right side and fit it onto the chair again. Adjust and rip and restitch any seams that are not perfect. Use a small ripping tool for this, being careful not to tear the fabric.

Finishing off the base of the cover

From the remnants, cut 4 pieces of fabric, each the length of one lower edge and each piece 7 inches deep.

Tip the chair on end so that you can see the underside and pin the pieces to the bottom edge of the cover, leaving a space around each chair leg. Turn under the short edges to make them neat. Stitch to the cover.

Make a turning along the remaining raw edge of each piece at least 1 inch deep. This will act as a casing.

Thread straight tape continuously through each casing and when the cover is in place pull the tape tight and tie it with a bow (figure **8**).

Laundering

Remove the cover and wash it carefully. When it is still slightly damp, replace it on the chair and iron it.

Curve back chairs

The method for making covers for curve back chairs is the same as for square back chairs, but there are no top or side edge pieces.

Piece 1 (the inside back) and piece 3 (the outside back) are pinned to each other, the corners of piece 1 are darted and shaped to fit the curve along the top of the chair back (figure **9**).

Cushions

If your chair has box cushions, these must be covered too. Measure the cushion carefully, from back to front and side to side. Measure the depth of the cushion at its sides and the perimeter of the top of the cushion.

The cushion top and base. Cut 2 pieces of fabric, each the same size and shape of the cushion top, plus 1 inch seam allowance all around.

The side strip. Cut a strip of fabric to the length of the perimeter of the top of the cushion plus 2 inches, and cut the width of this strip to the depth of the cushion at the side, plus 2 inches.

Cover piping cord with bias strip to double the length of the perimeter of the cushion top.

Place one of the pieces of fabric on the cushion top, wrong side facing you, and pin the strip to it so that the strip lies around the sides of the cushion. Pin the short ends of the strip together. Turn the cushion over and place the other piece on the cushion and pin its edges to the strip.

Insert the piping as before. When inserting the piping into the lower back seam pin it to one side of this seam only.

Remove the cover and stitch around all the seams.

The back opening. Leave the lower back seam open, finishing the raw edges there. Sew snap fastener tape along the back opening.

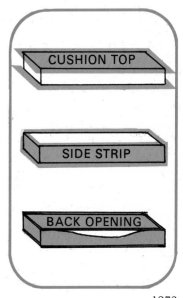

CUSHION TOP

SIDE STRIP

BACK OPENING

Tatting a pretty edging

Here is the handkerchief edging pattern illustrated in Tatting chapter 1, page 234. The square daisy motif is a perfect example of a design which can be worked to any dimension as a traycloth, tablecloth or even a bedspread. The squares are joined while working and then a final border is added.

Tatting with a ball thread

When tatting with two separate threads, provided there are no Josephine knots on the chains, it is quite possible to work with one thread on a shuttle and the second coming straight from the ball of cotton. This saves unnecessary winding, especially on a large project. Both the patterns given in this chapter can be worked either with two shuttles or with one shuttle and a ball thread.

Handkerchief edging

Materials you will need
☐ Coats and Clark's Tatting-Crochet, size 70, art. C21, 1 ball
☐ Shuttle(s)
☐ One No.12 or No.14 steel crochet hook
☐ Fabric for handkerchief, 9in by 9in

Size
To fit about 8½in square handkerchief

Working the edging
To work the straight part of the edging, begin with a ring of 4ds, p, 4ds, p, 4ds, close.
*Reverse work, ch of 4ds, p, 4ds.
Reverse work, r of 4ds, join

to last p of last r, 2ds, 6p each separated by 2ds, 4ds, close.
Reverse work, ch of 4ds, p, 4ds.
Reverse work, r of 4ds, join to last p of last r, 4ds, p, 4ds, close.*
Repeat from * to * 4 times more.
Work scallops as follows: **reverse work, ch of 4ds, p, 4ds. Large r of 5ds, p, 5ds, p, 5ds, p, 2ds, p, 5ds, close.
Reverse work, ch of 6ds, join to free p of last r but one, 2ds, 4p each separated by 2ds, 2ds.
Reverse work, small r of 7ds, join to last p of large r, 1ds, p, 6ds, close.
Reverse work, ch of 2ds, 6p each separated by 2ds, 2ds.
Reverse work, small r of 6ds, join to last p of small r, 1ds, join to next p of large r, 7ds, close.
Reverse work, ch of 2ds, 5p each separated by 2ds, 6ds.
Reverse work, join to next p of large r, ch of 4ds, p, 4ds.
Reverse work, r of 4ds, join to last p of last but one ch, 4ds, p, 4ds, close.**
Repeat from ** to ** once more, then repeat from * to * 5 times.
Work the corner scallops by repeating from ** to ** 3 times but omitting the ring and its following chain between each scallop. At the 2nd repeat (i.e. the corner), work the large ring as follows: 5ds, p, 5ds, p, 5ds, p, 2ds, p, 2ds, p, 5ds, close.
Work the following chain and ring and next chain in the usual way, then work a small ring as follows: 6ds, join to p of small r, 1ds, join to next p on large r, 1ds, p, 6ds, close.

Work an extra chain with 6 picots then complete scallop in the usual way.
Continue until the edging is complete, joining the final chain of the scallop following the 4th corner to the first ring of the edging.

To mount the edging
Cut the handkerchief to fit the tatting, allowing for a very narrow rolled hem. Work single crochet evenly over the hem by pushing the hook through the fabric.
Sew the tatting to the crochet with small overcast stitches through each single crochet, picking up the picots on the inner edge of the tatting.
The handkerchief illustrated is decorated in each corner with an appliqué clover leaf made of 3 small rings each of 12ds and worked close together.

▲ *Using ball thread and one shuttle*

Square motif daisy mat

Materials you will need
☐ Clark's Big Ball Mercerized Crochet No.10
☐ Shuttle(s)

Size
Each motif measures approximately 4in square. One ball of No.10 crochet cotton makes approximately 5½ motifs.

Working the motif
Work the center daisies with one shuttle.
Make r of 3ds, 9 long p each separated by 2ds, 3ds, close.
Do not leave a space but make another ring of 3ds, join to last p of last ring, 2ds, 8 long p each separated by 2ds, 3ds, close. Repeat from * to *

twice more, joining the last picot of the 4th ring to the first picot of the first ring. Cut and tie the ends to finish off.
Make three more daisies joining them into a square at the center picots of petals as shown.
Work the square edging with 2 shuttles.
Start at the corner with r of 5ds, p, 5ds, p, 5ds, p, 5ds, close. *Reverse work, ch of 8ds.
Reverse work, r of 5ds, join to last p of previous r, 5ds, p, 5ds, p, 5ds, close.
Reverse work, ch of 5ds, join to center p of free daisy petal as shown, 5ds.
Reverse work, make another ring like the last.
Reverse work, ch of 8ds.
Reverse work, make another ring as before.*
Repeat from * to *.
Work the corner by making another ring as before but joined close to the last without working a chain, to make a pair. Repeat from * to * again and continue all around the square, working pairs of rings at each corner and finishing by joining the last picot of the final ring to the first picot of the first ring. Cut and tie the ends to finish off.
The squares are joined together at the free picots on each ring of the edging, as shown.
Once the mat has been completed, work an outer border using two shuttles. Start half way along the side of any outer square motif. R of 5ds, p, 5ds, join to free p on square motif, 5ds, p, 5ds, close.
*Reverse work, ch of 2ds, 4p each separated by 2ds, 2ds.
Reverse work, r of 5ds, join to last p of previous r, 5ds, join to next r on square motif, 5ds, p, 5ds, close.*
Repeat from * to * along edge of mat but, at places where the square motifs join each other, leave one ring of the outer border unattached to the main part of the mat.
Turn the corners by working from * to * twice and joining both these rings to the picot which joins the corner pair of rings of the square motif.

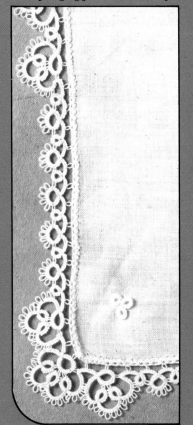

▼ *Pretty edging for a handkerchief* ▼ *Detail of the square daisy motif showing joining to adjacent motifs* ▲ *Motifs joined to make a long mat*

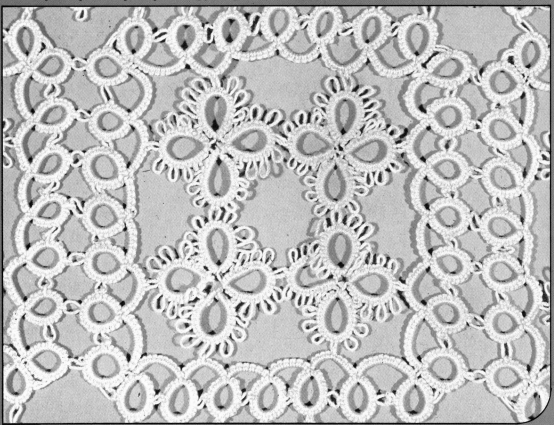

1275

Successful dressmaking with checks and stripes

A very important aspect of dressmaking is using a fabric to its best advantage, and making full use of checks and stripes is as exciting as creating a new design. Take a simple pattern, make it up cleverly in a checked or striped fabric, and the result is a garment with well projected detail.

Fixed fashion rules, such as lengthwise stripes for the large figure and checks for the small, have long been discarded. As long as the size of the design on the fabric is right for the proportions of the garment, and the proportions of the garment suit the wearer, there is no reason why large figures should not wear checks and small figures wear bold stripes.

This chapter gives advice on choosing the fabric and selecting the right style, and finishes with the all important aspects of cutting and fitting to help you achieve the best possible effect for your figure type.

▲ *Checks for Vogue by Dior*

Buying the fabric

Checks

With such a variety of checks available it is impossible to cover every aspect of making a purchase in one of these fabrics. However, there are some rules to observe which can be applied to most types of checks.

The main consideration must be matching the checks. So first look to see if the design is balanced (figure **1**). Does the color repeat regularly, or are there colors in the lengthwise weave which are not repeated in the crosswise weave or vice versa? If so, you must treat the fabric as you would for one way.

Also look to see if there are the same amount of threads in the lengthwise pattern as there are in the crosswise pattern. If there aren't, the fabric must again be considered as one way. And even if the same amount of threads have been used in each direction, one

thread gauge may be greater than the other, thereby making the pattern irregular. A check may even look regular when in fact it isn't. Dressmaking chapter 22, page 436, shows you how you can make a simple test to find out.

Stripes

The first consideration is the repeat of the design. This can create width if the pattern is bold and the colors show an obviously wide pattern repeat. For a slim look, the stripes should not be spaced too far apart.

Striped fabrics are made in two ways—horizontal and vertical. If you want to combine horizontal and vertical stripes in one garment, make sure they are designed well and make an interesting combination.

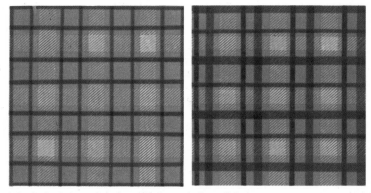

▲ **1.** *Left: balanced design; Right: unbalanced design*

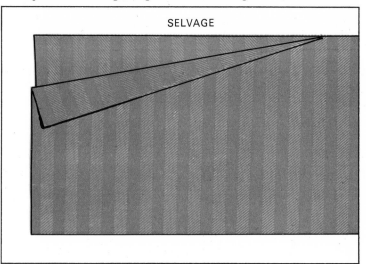

SELVAGE

▲ **2.** *Distortion on the selvages of a striped fabric*

Checking the fabric finish

As the fabric is unrolled on the shop counter, lift one selvage and see if the corresponding selvage meets it correctly. Look at the stripes and checks and see if the finish has distorted the pattern on the cloth so that they do not meet from side to side (figure **2**). Although some of these fabrics can be folded quite easily after the length has been cut off, others are very resistant to folding since they have been carelessly finished and dragged. Here one side is so much out of line it cannot be used with any success.

If you are in doubt, a good assistant who is familiar with the merchandise should be able to advise you. If, however, you cannot get assurance, buying the fabric could lead to disappointment.

Far right: wide stripes perfectly aligned, Vogue Pattern; Top right: effective use of checks on a cape coat, Vogue Pattern by Givenchy; Right: checks bias cut on a skirt, Vogue Pattern

Choosing the right style

Checks and stripes have an all-over geometrical and predictable design. But the figure shapes they have to cover have rounded contours which are quite unpredictable. Since every figure is different, it is not possible to design an ideal checked or striped pattern for all figures. It is up to each dressmaker therefore to choose her style, at the same time observing the few golden rules given below.

O Use large checks or wide stripes on large areas uncluttered by detail. Never distort the geometry of the design with unnecessary breaks, seams or darts. Only use them if they actually enhance the style and the design of the fabric. Figures **3** and **4** show a good and bad usage of large checks.

O Avoid darts as much as possible. A wrongly placed dart will cut or distort the design. If darts are unavoidable, try to move them so that one side of the dart seamline remains in the straight or the crosswise grain of the fabric.

O Rounded edges on collars, cuffs and pockets are not suitable for all types of checks or stripes. Confine them to small checks and fine stripes.

O Closely fitted garments, such as dresses and tailored suits, look best in small to medium sized checks.

O If the style has lots of detail such as pockets, yoke, collar, it is best to use small checks, otherwise the detail will be lost in the background of the fabric.

Designing for checks and stripes

A clever dressmaker can have fun designing for these fabrics. The illustrations in this chapter give ideas for styles which show checks and stripes to advantage.

A simple and most effective idea is to choose a fabric with light and dark alternating colors which are repeated regularly. Make a pleated skirt using the dark sections for the pleat distance and the light sections for the pleat depth. As the pleats spring open, the light color is revealed, creating a pretty striped effect.

Cutting notes

Be prepared; making a garment in checks and stripes takes longer than making a garment in other fabrics. Attention to detail starts on the cutting table where you must take great care to match the design. Be especially careful when cutting the long sections where a mistake could be disastrous.

Before cutting make the necessary adjustments to the length and width of the

▲ *Vogue by Fabiani, band cross checked*

pattern and do not take a chance by adding or cutting off the pattern on the layout.

When pinning down the pattern, make sure that all corresponding pattern pieces are pinned in the same check or stripe. Start matching from the hem upward (figure **5**). If matched from the underarm section downward, any ease or side bust dart would throw the pattern out of line. If you are not sure what adjustments will be necessary to the side bust darts, add 2 inches to the hemline at the Back and add extra seam allowance to the armhole line. Then, should you have to lift fabric into the dart, you will have enough

▲ **3.** *A good choice of style for large checks*

▲ **4.** *An unsuitable style choice for large checks*

length to re-cut the Back line up the fabric pattern.

Matching checks and stripes for set-in sleeves is often difficult, especially if severe adjustments have been made to the armhole line at the fitting.

To allow you some play on the sleeve crown, cut the whole sleeve cap with at least 1 inch seam allowance (figure **6**). Be sure to mark out the seamline around the sleeve cap carefully so that if you should have to let out on the sleeve crown, you will be able to compensate on the underarm to avoid a large armhole.

Yokes, pocket flaps and collars must always be cut with special care (figure **7**).

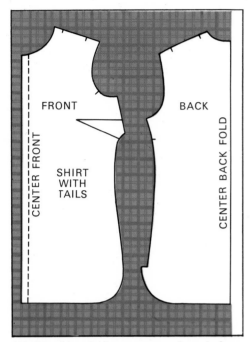

▲ 5. *Matching checks on a pattern from the hem*

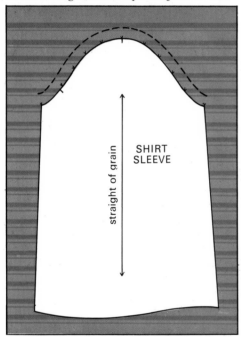

▲ 6. *Cutting 1 inch seams on a sleeve cap*

Make sure that the checked or striped pattern continues through the pocket or yoke. Tilted pockets must be adjusted precisely to the straight of the grain line on the pattern so that, although the pocket is cut on the cross, the pattern continues across the garment.

When cutting a collar from prominent colored checks or stripes, lay the complete collar pattern on the fabric to see that the colors repeat on both collar ends similarly. If not, it is best to cut the collar in two halves with a Center Back seam, making sure that the pattern lines coincide. Careful attention to detail is important.

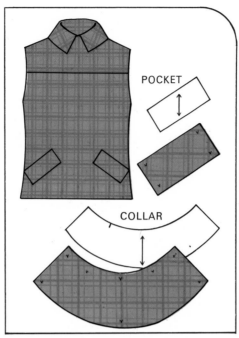

▲ 7. *Matching checks on yoke, pockets and collar*

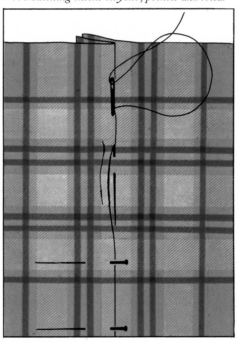

▲ 8. *Slip-basting a seam*

Preparing for fitting

Mark out the pattern detail with care since fitting alterations on these fabrics are movements of consequence. Altering one section may make it out of line with a corresponding section which must then also be adjusted to realign the pattern.

Baste the sections together quite firmly and gently press the seam allowance to get as smooth a fit as possible for the first fitting.

Slip-basting

It is often difficult to match the straight grain lines of vertical seams such as the

Center Back seam in a skirt. This can be made easier with slip-basting.

Slip-basting is a method of basting where one side of the seam edge is folded on the outside of the fabric along the straight of grain line and brought to meet the other seamline in the corresponding grain line. To baste the seam together, work through the folded edge into the flat fabric as shown, slip-basting along with small stitches (figure **8**).

Although slip-basting will help you match the lengthwise grain lines, do not rely on it to give you enough anchorage for matching the horizontal lines of the fabric pattern. You cannot control the tension of the basting stitches well enough, and after slip-basting it is always necessary to pin or rebaste from the inside, having laid the fabric flat.

Shaped seams

Pinning and basting shaped seams requires a great deal of care. Since the seam runs through the bias of the fabric it is so easy to accidentally drag the seam edge.

Use pins at right angles to the seamline to give you extra control over the edge and allow you to pin together matching pattern lines.

Fitting

The obvious lengthwise and crosswise grain lines and pattern lines are your fitting guide. Make sure they hang well and are not tilted or dragged to one side. Directional design will emphasize deviation, and figure faults are more obvious.

But if the fabric design is cleverly adjusted and incorporated into the fitting of the garment without affecting the straight and crosswise directional pattern, you will see that your dress allows you to forget your problems.

It is often said that the waist seam and hem must continue in the pattern line. This, of course, is wrong. If a figure fault makes the straight waist pucker, it is essential that the fullness is taken off into the waist seam. But always check that the crosswise grain continues around the figure perfectly horizontally.

Allow the waist seam to follow your natural waistline and to hide the adjustment make a belt wide enough to suit you. When making the hem, remember that the checks or stripes will only go straight around the hem if the garment is cut perfectly straight from hips to hemline. If the skirt is cut with a flare, however slight, your hemline will be rounded and not run in the line of the fabric pattern.

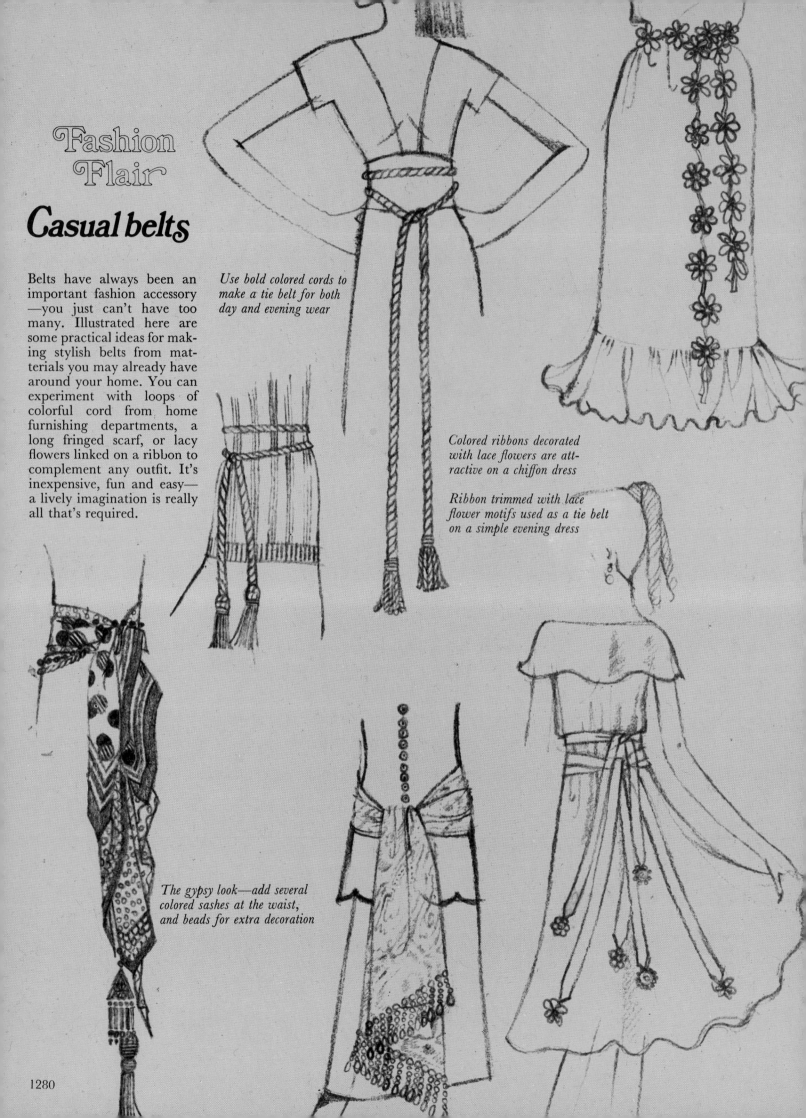

Fashion Flair

Casual belts

Belts have always been an important fashion accessory —you just can't have too many. Illustrated here are some practical ideas for making stylish belts from matterials you may already have around your home. You can experiment with loops of colorful cord from home furnishing departments, a long fringed scarf, or lacy flowers linked on a ribbon to complement any outfit. It's inexpensive, fun and easy— a lively imagination is really all that's required.

Use bold colored cords to make a tie belt for both day and evening wear

Colored ribbons decorated with lace flowers are attractive on a chiffon dress

Ribbon trimmed with lace flower motifs used as a tie belt on a simple evening dress

The gypsy look—add several colored sashes at the waist, and beads for extra decoration

Pattern Library

The fisherwomen

Beads and sequins can be used to great effect combined with embroidery, either as a main part of the design or, as in this embroidered panel, to add highlights to a particular area. The embroidery is worked in outline stitch for the outlines, and outline stitch filling has been used for the details. The mesh of the net is created by couching, and the sequins scattered in the net depict the catch of fish. The scales on the larger fish are highlighted with further sequins.

Monkeying about with shaping

This most cunning of monkey people is not only a delightful toy to make but is a good example of the superb effects which can be achieved with shaping in knitting.

Size

About 20in high.

Gauge

6 sts and 8 rows to 1in over st st worked on No.3 needles using Mohair.
6½ sts and 8½ rows to 1in over st st worked on No.3 needles using Germantown.

Materials

Bernat Mohair Plus, 3x1½oz balls in main color A
Bernat Berella Germantown, 1x2oz ball in contrast color B
One pair No.3 needles (or Canadian No.10)
Stuffing
One pair glass eyes
NB For a young child it is safer to use felt for eyes

Body back

Using No.3 needles and A, cast on 35 sts.
Work in reversed st st (see Knitting Know-how chapter 3) beg with a P row.
Work 16 rows.
17th row P10, P2 tog, P11, P2 tog, P10. Work 5 rows.
23rd row P2 tog, P8, P2 tog, P9, P2 tog, P8, P2 tog. Work 5 rows.
29th row P2 tog, (P7, P2 tog) 3 times. Work 13 rows.
43rd row P7, inc in next st, P8, inc in next st, P8. Work 7 rows.
51st row P7, inc in next st,

Knitting Know-how 65

P10, inc in next st, P8.
Work 7 rows.
59th row P7, inc in next st, P12, inc in next st, P8.
Work 3 rows.

Shape shoulders

Bind off 3 sts at beg of next 6 rows.
Work 4 rows on rem sts for neck.
Bind off.

Body front

Work as given for Back.
Seam Back and Front on wrong side leaving neck open for stuffing.

Arms

Using No.3 needles and A, cast on 17 sts.
Work in reversed st st beg with a P row. Work 12 rows.
Inc one st at each end of next and every following 12th row until there are 25 sts.
Work 11 rows. Bind off.
Work second arm in same way.
Fold each arm in half and seam leaving cast-on edges open.

Legs

Using No.3 needles and A, cast on 22 sts.
Work in reversed st st beg with a P row. Work 8 rows.
Inc one st at each end of next and every following 8th row until there are 32 sts.
Work 3 rows.
Bind off.
Work second leg in same way.
Fold each leg in half and seam leaving cast-on edges open.

Head

Using No.3 needles and A, cast on 23 sts.
Work in reversed st st beg with a P row.
Work 2 rows.
Inc one st at each end of every P row until there are 29 sts. K 1 row.
9th row P13, inc in each of next 2 sts, P to end.
K 1 row.
11th row P14, inc in each of next 2 sts, P to end.
K 1 row.
13th row P15, inc in each of next 2 sts, P to end.
Work 3 rows.
17th row P4, inc in next st, P11, inc in each of next 2 sts, P11, inc in next st, K5.
Work 3 rows.
21st row P5, inc in next st, P12, inc in each of next 2 sts, P12, inc in next st, P6.
Work 15 rows.

Shape head top

1st row P6, P2 tog, P11, P2 tog, P1, P2 tog, P11, P2 tog, P6.
Work 5 rows.
7th row P5, P2 tog, P10, P2 tog, P1, P2 tog, P10, P2 tog, P5.
Work 3 rows.
11th row Inc in first st, P3, P2 tog, P9, P2 tog, P1, P2 tog, P9, P2 tog, P2, inc in next st, P1.
Work 3 rows.
15th row Inc in first st, P3, P2 tog, P6, P2 tog twice, P1, P2 tog twice, P6, P2 tog, P2, inc in next st, P1.
16th row K12, K2 tog, K1, K2 tog, K12.
17th row Inc in first st, P8, P2 tog twice, P1, P2 tog twice, P7, inc in next st, P1.
Bind off.
Fold bound-off edge in half and seam forming crown of head.

Upper face

Eye backing

Using No.3 needles and B, cast on 5 sts.
Work in st st beg with a K row.
Work 5 rows. Break yarn.
Slip sts on holder until required.

Work second piece in same way.

Face

Using No.3 needles and B, cast on 15 sts.
Work in st st beg with a K row.
Work 2 rows.
3rd row K1, K up 1 tbl by lifting the yarn before the next st and knitting into the back of this loop to inc one st, K to last st, K up 1 tbl, K1.
4th row P to end. Rep last 2 rows until there are 25 sts.

Shape eyelids

1st row K5, K up 1 tbl, K3, K up 1 tbl, K9, K up 1 tbl, K3, K up 1 tbl, K5.
2nd row P.
3rd row K5, K up 1 tbl, K5, K up 1 tbl, K9, K up 1 tbl, K5, K up 1 tbl, K5.
4th row P.
5th row K2 tog, K3, bind off 7 sts for first eyelid, K to last 12 sts, bind off 7sts for second eyelid, K3, K2 tog.
6th row P4, P5 across first eye backing, P9, P5 across second eye backing, P4.
7th row K8, K2 tog, K7, K2 tog, K8. P 1 row.
Dec one st at each end of next and following K row.
P 1 row.

Increase for upper lip

1st row (K4, K up 1 tbl) twice, K2, K up 1 tbl, K3, K up 1 tbl, K2, (K up 1 tbl, K4) twice. Work 3 rows.
5th row (K4, K up 1 tbl) 3 times, K5, (K up 1 tbl, K4) 3 times.
P 1 row.

Shape upper lip

1st row K30, ytf, sl 1. Turn.
2nd row Ytf, sl 1, P25, sl 1. Turn.
3rd row Ytf, sl 1, ytb, K21, ytf, sl 1. Turn.
4th row Ytf, sl 1, P17, sl 1. Turn.
5th row Ytf, sl 1, ytb, K15, ytf, sl 1. Turn.
6th row Ytf, sl 1, P13, sl 1. Turn.
7th row Ytf, sl 1, ytb, K to end of row.
8th row P across all sts. Bind off.

Lower face

Using No.3 needles and B, with RS of Upper face facing, K up the loops from just beyond the bound-off edge on WS of Upper face. Pick up and K33 sts from behind the bound-off edge as the bound-off edge itself is used to mark the lip line. P 1 row.
2nd row K2 tog, K to last 2 sts, K2 tog. Work 5 rows.
8th row K2, (K2 tog, K3) 5 times, K2 tog, K2. Work 3 rows.
12th row K2 tog twice, (K2, K2 tog) twice, K1, (K2 tog, K2) twice, K2 tog twice. P 1 row.
14th row K2 tog, (K1, K2 tog) 5 times. Bind off.
Sew head section around sides of Upper and Lower face with seamed bound-off edges forming point at center top of face. Leave neck edges (cast-on edge of Head and bound-off edge of Lower face) open for stuffing.

Hands

Using No.3 needles and B, cast on 17 sts.
Work in st st beg with a K row. Work 6 rows.
7th row K1, K up 1 tbl, K6, K up 1 tbl, K3, K up 1 tbl, K6, K up 1 tbl, K1. P 1 row.
9th row K8, K up 1 tbl, K5, K up 1 tbl, K8. P 1 row.
11th row K1, K up 1 tbl, (K7, K up 1 tbl) 3 times, K1. P 1 row.
13th row K18, turn.
14th row P9, turn.
Work on these 9 sts for thumb. Work 5 rows.
Last row *P2 tog, rep from * to end of row. Thread yarn through rem sts and draw up. Seam thumb.
With RS facing, attach yarn to rem 8 sts, K to end. P 1 row across all sts. 18 sts.
Next row K1, K up 1 tbl, K to last st, K up 1 tbl, K1. Work 5 rows.
Bind off 3 sts at beg of next 4 rows. Bind off rem sts.
Fold hand in half and seam along top and side.
Make second hand in same manner.

Feet

Using No.3 needles and B, cast on 21 sts.
Work in st st beg with a K row. Work 10 rows.
11th row K1, K up 1 tbl, K8, K up 1 tbl, K3, K up 1 tbl, K8, K up 1 tbl, K1. P 1 row.
13th row K10, K up 1 tbl, K5, K up 1 tbl, K10. P1 row.
15th row K1, K up 1 tbl, K9, K up 1 tbl, K7, K up 1 tbl, K9, K up 1 tbl, K1. P 1 row.
17th row K20. Turn.
18th row P9. Turn.
Work on these 9 sts for toe. Work 7 rows.
Last row *P2 tog, rep from * to end of row. Thread yarn through rem sts and draw up. Seam toe.
With RS facing, attach yarn to rem sts and K to end. P 1 row.
Next row K1, K up 1 tbl, K to last st, K up 1 tbl, K1. Work 7 rows.
Bind off 4 sts at beg of next 4 rows. Bind off.
Fold foot in half and seam along bound-off edge and side. Make second foot in same manner.

Ears

Using No.3 needles and B, cast on 5 sts.
Work in st st beg with a K row. Work 2 rows.
3rd row K1, (K up 1 tbl, K1) 4 times.
4th row P.
5th row K3, (K up 1 tbl, K3) twice. Bind off.
Make 2nd ear in same manner.

Tail

Using No.3 needles and A, cast on 17 sts.
Work in reversed st st beg with a P row. Work 12 rows.
Dec one st at each end of next and every following 8th row until 5 sts rem.
Work 7 rows. Break yarn and thread through rem sts. Draw up.
Seam tail leaving cast-on edge open. If the seam is drawn tight at the narrow end it will make the tail curl upward slightly.

▲ *A mischievous monkey to knit in fuzzy mohair and plain yarn*

Finishing

Stuff limbs, body, head and tail. Sew head to neck, and arms, legs and tail to body. Stuff feet and hands slightly and sew on. Curl ears around cast-on edge and sew in place. Sew glass or felt eyes beneath eyelids. A little stuffing behind the felt looks more life-like. Embroider two lazy daisy stitches at either side of nose for nostrils on upper face as shown in the illustration.

Ski sweaters for teenagers

Basic Wardrobe Knitting

Give this attractive and practical basic sweater a different look by knitting stripes of contrasting colors around the sleeves.

Sizes

Directions are for 26in chest. The figures in brackets [ ] refer to the 28, 30 and 32in sizes respectively.
Length at center back, 15½ [17¼:19:20¼]in.
Sleeve seam, 11½[12½:14:16]in or as required.

Gauge
6½ sts and 8½ rows to 1in over st st worked on No.4 needles.

Materials
Sports yarn
For either design including caps, 4[5:5:6] 2oz skeins of main color A
1 skein of first contrast B
1 skein of second contrast C
One pair No.3 needles (or Canadian No.10)
One pair No.4 needles (or Canadian No.9)
One set of 4 No.3 double pointed needles
One No.D (3.00 mm) crochet hook for st st cap edging.

Plain sleeved version

Front

Using No.3 needles and A, cast on 99[105:111:117] sts. Work 16 rows of K1, P1 rib. Change to No.4 needles and st st beg with a K row.
Work until 10[11½:13:14]in or desired length to underarm, ending with a P row.

Shape armholes
Bind off 3[4:4:5] sts at beg of next 2 rows.
Bind off 3[3:4:4] sts at beg of next 2 rows.
Bind off 3 sts at beg of next 2 rows.
Bind off 2 sts at beg of next 2 rows.
Bind off 1 st at beg of next 2 rows.
Work without shaping until armholes measure 3[3¼:3½:3¾] in, ending with a P row.
Inc one st at each end of next row.
Work without further shaping until armholes measure 3¾[4: 4½:4½]in, ending with a P row.

Shape neck
1st row K31[32:33:34]. Turn. Complete left shoulder on these sts.
*Bind off at neck edge 4 sts once, 3 sts every other row twice and 2 sts once, then 1 st every other row twice.
Work without shaping until armhole measures 5[5¼:5½: 5¾]in, ending at armhole edge.

Shape shoulder
Bind off 4 sts every other row 4 times; then 1[2:3:4] sts once.*
With RS facing, slip center 15[17:19:21] sts onto holder until required for neckband.
Attach A to rem sts and K to end of row.
P 1 row.
Complete as for other shoulder from * to *.

Back

Using No.3 needles and A, cast on 85[91:97:103] sts. Work as given for Front until same length to armholes, ending with a P row.

Shape armholes
Bind off 2[3:3:4] sts at beg of next 2 rows.
Bind off 2[2:3:3] sts at beg of next 2 rows.
Bind off 1 st at beg of next 6 rows.
Work without shaping until armholes measure 3[3¼:3½:3¾] in, ending with a P row.
Inc one st at each end of next row.
Work without further shaping until armholes measure 4½ [4¾:5:5¼]in, ending with a P row.

Shape neck
1st row K22[23:24:25]. Turn. Work right Back shoulder on these sts.
2nd row Bind off 3 sts, work to end of row.
Work 1 row.
4th row Bind off 2 sts, work to end of row.
Work until armhole measures same length as Front to shoulder, ending at armhole edge.

Shape shoulder
Work as given for Front.**
With RS facing, slip center 29[31:33:35] sts onto holder.
Attach yarn to rem sts and K to end of row.
Work 1 row.
Complete as for other shoulder working from ** to **

Sleeves

Using No.3 needles and A, cast on 40[42:44:46] sts.
Work 16 rows of K1, P1 rib.
Change to No.4 needles and st st, beg with a K row and inc 6 times evenly across the first row.
Inc one st at each end of 3rd and every 8th row until there are 66[70:74:78] sts.
Work without shaping until sleeve measures 11½[12½:14:16] in or desired length, ending with a P row.

Shape cap
Bind off 3[3:4:4] sts at beg of next 2 rows.
Bind off 2 sts at beg of next 2 rows.
Bind off 1 st at beg of next and every row until 38 sts rem.
Bind off 3 sts at beg of next 2 rows.
Bind off rem sts.

Shoulder edging

Using No.3 needles and B, with RS of Front facing, pick up and K19[20:21:22] sts along bound-off shoulder edge.
Work 3 rows of K1, P1 rib.
Break off B.
Change to C and K 1 row.
Work 3 rows of K1, P1 rib.
Bind off in rib.
Work other shoulder in same manner.
Join Front shoulders to Back shoulders.

Neckband

Using set of 4 No.3 needles and B, pick up and K10 sts to Back holder, K sts from holder, pick up and K10 sts to shoulder seam, pick up and K20 sts down Front neck, K sts from holder and pick up and K20 sts up other side of neck.
Work 3 rows of K1, P1 rib.
Break off B.
Change to C and K 1 row.
Work 3 rows of K1, P1 rib.
Bind off in rib.

Cap

Using set of 4 No.3 needles and A, cast on 104[112:120:128] sts and divide on 3 needles.
Work 4 rows of K1, P1 rib.
Using B, P 1 row.
Work 3 rows of K1, P1 rib.
Break off B.
Using C, P 1 row.
Work 3 rows of K1, P1 rib.
Break off C.
Continue in st st, beg with a P row.
Work 8 rows.
Continue in st st, working the next row K in order to reverse the surface having completed the turn back edge.
Work 5in more without shaping.
1st dec round *K2 tog, K11[12:13:14], rep from * to end.
Work 3 rows.

2nd dec row *K2 tog, K10 [11:12:13], rep from * to end.
Work 3 rows.
Continue dec in this way on next and every following 4th row until 5 dec rounds have been worked then on every other round until 16 sts rem. Thread yarn through rem sts, draw up. Finish off ends. Fold brim back at fold line. Work 1 round sc along this edge.

Striped sleeve version

Back and Front

Work as given for Plain sleeved version.

Striped sleeves

Work as given for Plain sleeves inc 10 times evenly across first row of st st and inc until there are 62[66:70: 74] sts.
P 1 row.

Work stripe
Using B, K 1 row.
Work 3 rows of K1, P1 rib.
Break off B.
Using C, K 1 row.
Work 3 rows of K1, P1 rib.
Break off C.
Complete sleeve using A only.

Divide for vertical stripe
1st row K28[30:32:34]. Turn.
Complete first half of cap on these sts.
P 1 row.
Inc one st at side edge on next and following 8th row. 30[32:34:36] sts.
Work until sleeve measures 11½[12½:14:16]in, ending at side edge.

Shape cap
Bind off 3[3:4:4] sts at beg of next row.
Work 1 row.
Bind off 2 sts at beg of next row.
Work 1 row.
Dec 1 st at beg of next and every other row until 16 sts rem.
Bind off 3 sts at beg of next row.
Work 1 row. Bind off rem sts.

▲ *Two versions of the ski sweater, one with striped sleeves, the other with plain, both with matching caps*

With RS of work facing, bind off center 6 sts using a short length of C.
Attach A to rem sts and work to correspond to other side. Work second sleeve in the same manner.
Shoulder and sleeve stripe
Sew sleeves to Back and Front armholes.
Using No.3 needles and B, with RS of Front facing, pick up and K62[66:70:74] sts along shoulder and sleeve division. Work 3 rows of K1, P1 rib. Break off B.
Change to C and K1 row.
Work 3 rows of K1, P1 rib.
Bind off in rib.
Seam stripe to Back sleeve and shoulder edges.

Collar

Using set of 4 No.3 needles and A, pick up and K sts as given for Neckband.

Work 3½[3¾:4:4] of K1, P1 rib.
Break off A.
Change to C and P 1 row.
Work 3 rows of K1, P1 rib.
Break off C.
Change to B and P 1 row.
Work 3 rows of K1, P1 rib.
Bind off in rib.

Cap

Using set of 4 No.3 needles and B, cast on 112[112:128: 123] sts and divide on 3 needles.
Work 3 rounds of K1, P1 rib.
Change to B and P 1 round.
Work 3 rounds of K1, P1 rib.
Change to C and P 1 round.
Work 3 rounds of K1, P1 rib.
Change to A and P 1 round.
Continue in rib using A only.
Work 5½[5½:6:6]in.
1st dec round Rib 6, *sl 1, K2 tog, psso, rib 11[11:13:13], rep from * to last 5[5:7:7] sts,

rib to end.
Rib 8 rounds.
2nd dec round Rib 5, *P3 tog, rib 10[10:12:12], rep from * to last 5[5:7:7] sts, rib to end.
Continue dec in this way on every 9th round until 5 dec rounds have been worked.
Work 3 rounds more.
Last round *P3 tog, sl 1, K2 tog, psso, rep from * to end.
Thread yarn through rem sts and draw up. Finish off ends. Make a pompon using A and sew to center top.

Finishing

Press lightly.

Plain sleeved version
Join side and sleeve seams. Sew in sleeves.

Striped sleeve version
Join side and sleeve seams.

1285

Holders for bottles and glasses

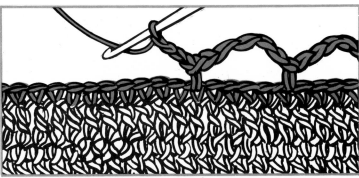

▲ *Working chain loops on the second row of contrast*

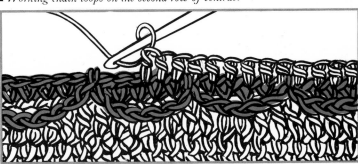

▲ *Holding loops forward*　　　▼ *Glass holder to match decanter*

The attractive surface pattern is achieved by catching up loops worked in contrast color yarn.

Sizes
Glass holder base, about 3in diameter.
Bottle holder base, about 4in diameter.
The sizes may be altered by using a smaller or larger crochet hook.

Gauge
8dc to 1in worked with No.C crochet hook.

Materials
Coats & Clark's O.N.T. Pearl Cotton
6 (50yd) balls main color A, white
1 ball contrast B, red
1 ball contrast C, blue
One No.C (2.50 mm) crochet hook
This quantity will make 4 glass holders and one bottle holder. Any change in size will alter the quantities required

Glass holder

Using No.C hook and A, ch5. Join with a ss into first ch to form circle.

1st round Ch1, work 11sc into circle. Join with a ss into first ch.

2nd round Ch3, 1dc into same st, *2dc into next st, rep from * to end. Join with a ss into 3rd of 3ch. 24dc including first ch as 1dc.

3rd round Ch1, 2sc in next dc, *1sc in next dc, 2sc in next dc, rep from * to end of round.
Join with a ss into first ch.

4th round Ch3, 1dc in next sc, 2dc in next sc, *1dc in each of next 2sc, 2dc in next sc, rep from * to end of round, join with a ss into 3rd of 3ch.

5th round Ch1, 1sc in each of next 2dc, 2sc in next dc, *1sc in each of next 3dc, 2sc in next dc, rep from * to end of round, join with a ss into first ch. 60sc including first ch.

6th round Ch3, 1dc in each of next 3sc, 2dc in next sc, *1dc in each of next 4sc, 2dc in next sc, rep from * to end of round, join with a ss into 3rd of 3ch. Finish off A.

7th round Using B, join with a ss into first dc, 1sc in each st to end of round. Join with a ss into first ch. 72sc including first ch.

8th round *Ch7, skip 5sc and work 1sc into next sc, rep from * to end of round. Join with a ss into first ch. 12 loops. Finish off B.

9th round Using A, join with a ss into first st inside loop, ch3, 1dc into each of next 4dc skipped in making first loop, *1dc into each of next 5dc skipped in making next loop holding loop forward so that it is not caught in, rep from * to end of round, join with a ss into 3rd of 3ch.

10th round Ch1, *1sc in next dc, rep from * to end of round, join with a ss into first ch. 60sc including first ch.

11th round Ch1, 1sc in next sc, 1sc in next st picking up center of B loop left on front of work, *1sc in each of next 4sc, 1sc in next st picking up front loop, rep from * to last 2 sts, 1sc in each st, join with a ss into first ch.

12th round Ch1, 1sc in each

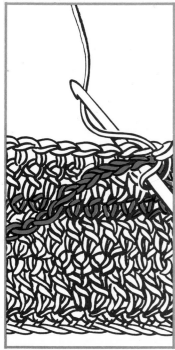

▲ *Catching loops up*

st to end, join with a ss into first ch. Finish off A.

13th round Using C, join with a ss into first st, ch1, 1sc in each st to end of round, join with a ss into first ch. 60sc including first ch.

14th round *Ch7, skip 4sc, 1sc in next sc, rep from * to end of round, join with a ss into first ch. Finish off C.

15th round Using A, join with a ss into first st, ch3, work as for 9th round working 4dc in 4 skipped sc of previous round. 48dc including 3ch.

16th round Ch1, *1sc in next st, rep from * to end of round. 48sc including first ch.

17th round As 11th.

18th round As 12th.

19th round *Ch3, 1sc in first of 3ch to form picot, 1sc in each of next 2sc, rep from * to end of round, join with a ss into first picot. Run in ends.

Bottle holder

Work as for glass holder but increase the base size by working 1st—6th round once then rep 5th and 6th rounds once more.

Work sides in same manner, working extra band in B so that there are 3 rows of loop patt, each row having 16 loops instead of 12.

Introduction to beading

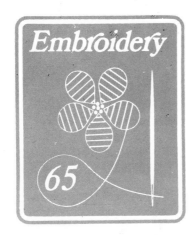

Methods and materials used for modern bead embroidery.

Materials and equipment

Thread

Cotton or silk thread is used for bead embroidery, and should be of the finest and strongest quality available. Before use, the thread is drawn once across beeswax and is used double thickness. Generally, in beadwork, the thread should not show on the right side of the work and a color suited to both the background fabric and the beads should be chosen.

Needles

Beading needles are long and fine and are available in sizes 10 to 13.

Frame

A hoop is generally advisable for working beading and is essential for tambour beading, both hands being left free for working—one hand using the hook and the other setting the beads.

Beads and sequins

There are many different types of beads and sequins available, each in a wide range of colors and sizes. Sequin material, which can be cut into pieces and various shapes, is obtainable in sheets of 12ft 6in lengths, about 2 feet wide. Sequin waste, the material left over after sequins have been cut out, is useful; it is about 3 inches wide and is available in lengths.

1288

Applying beadwork designs

Designs are marked out on the background fabric in the same way as for embroidery. Mark designs on the right side for hand stitched beading and on the wrong side for tambour beading. Beading should always be worked on the pieces of a garment before they are joined together. For perfectly worked seams, work the beading up to the seamline. Stitch the garment seam by hand, and if there are any gaps showing in the beading, fill in the odd beads.

Methods of beading

Six methods of attaching beads and sequins to the background fabric are given. The illustrations and diagrams show beads and sequins applied in straight lines, but design lines can, of course, curve, and can be broken or added to. The tension of the stitches used for beading should be firm but not too tight or the effect is spoiled. Make sure that the thread is fastened off securely at both ends of a row of beads.

Method 1

Bring the needle through to the front of the work and pick up one bead. Slide it along the needle and just onto the thread. Pick up one thread of the background fabric, the length of the bead along the design line. Draw the needle through the fabric to place the bead on the fabric and pick up the second bead.

Method 2

This method requires two needles and thread in use at the same time. Needle No.1, the beading needle, picks up two or more beads and stitches them to the fabric (following the technique in method 1). Needle No.2 then works the second stage, making a small slanting stitch between each bead, catching down the linking thread.

Method 3

Bring the needle up through the hole of the sequin, set the sequin on the fabric and take a tiny stitch to the side of it on the line of design. Bring the needle up through the next sequin and continue to the end of the line. This results in a scale-like effect.

Method 4

Bring the needle up through the hole in the first sequin. Set the next sequin on the fabric and insert the needle. Set the third sequin on the fabric and bring the needle up through the hole and then, making a backstitch, into the hole of the previous sequin. Continue applying further sequins using a backstitch each time.

Method 5

Each sequin is sewn to the fabric with a single backstitch, and again a contrasting thread can be used.

Method 6

Each sequin is held in place by a small bead which must be larger than the hole in the sequin. Bring the needle up through the hole, pick up a bead on the needle and insert the needle back through the hole in the sequin. Bring the needle up through the hole of the next sequin and continue in this way.

Tambour beading

This is a method of attaching beads and sequins by means of a small, sharp hook in a holder. The same method is used as that described for tambour work in Embroidery 14, p. 268. Set the fabric in the frame with the wrong side uppermost. Thread the beads onto a spool of thread—they can be threaded in a pattern sequence if required. Hold the hook in the right hand above the hoop, the left hand holding the thread, and flick up a bead beyond the hook as each stitch is made. For a "speckled" effect, flick up a bead for every second stitch only. Tambour beading is an especially good method for attaching small beads, bugles and sequins if the pattern is linear. Try combining tambour beading with hand stitched beading to achieve even more unusual effects.

Beaded cuffs

To bead two cuffs you will need:

- [ ] Sheet of sequin material measuring 2ft 6in by 2ft
- [ ] 2½mm gold pearls
- [ ] 5mm cup sequins in coral shade
- [ ] Yellow chalk beads
- [ ] 5mm flat sequins in blue-green shade
- [ ] White chalk beads
- [ ] Gold beads
- [ ] Small size pale blue chalk beads
- [ ] Sewing thread (cotton or silk)
- [ ] Beading needle

Working the cuffs

Prepare the thread by dragging it through a block of beeswax. Thread the needle with double thread. Mark the oblong shapes on the sequin material, using a fine ball point pen and a ruler. The size of the shapes can be adjusted to fit the depth of the cuff and the measurement around the wrist. Cut out the shapes with a pair of sharp scissors and pierce the holes with a pin, holding the sequin shape over a soft felt pad. All the beads, sequins and sequin shapes are sewn on by passing the thread through a small bead on top (method 6). Complete all the beadwork before making the cuff and attaching it to the sleeve.

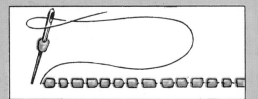

▲ *Method 1. Each bead stitched down separately*

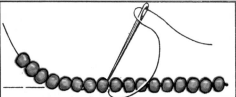

▲ *Method 2. Working two or more beads*

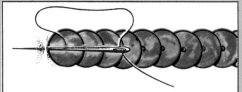

▲ *Method 3. Scale effect with sequins*

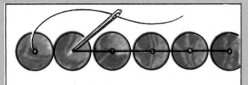

▲ *Method 4. Applying sequins with backstitch*

▲ *Method 5. Sequins sewn with single backstitch*

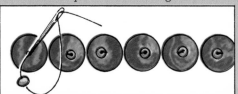

▲ *Method 6. Sequin held with a small bead*

◄ *Shimmering effect of toned beads and sequins*

▼ *Diagram for working the beaded cuff*

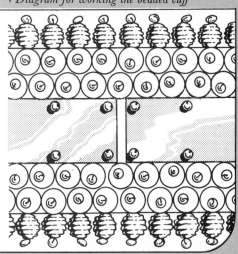

Coral 5mm cup sequin — yellow chalk bead.
Blue/green 5mm flat sequin — white chalk
bead.

Gold oblong shape cut from large sheet
attached by 2½mm gold pearls.

Gold beads attached with small pale blue
chalk bead — sewn on fold line.

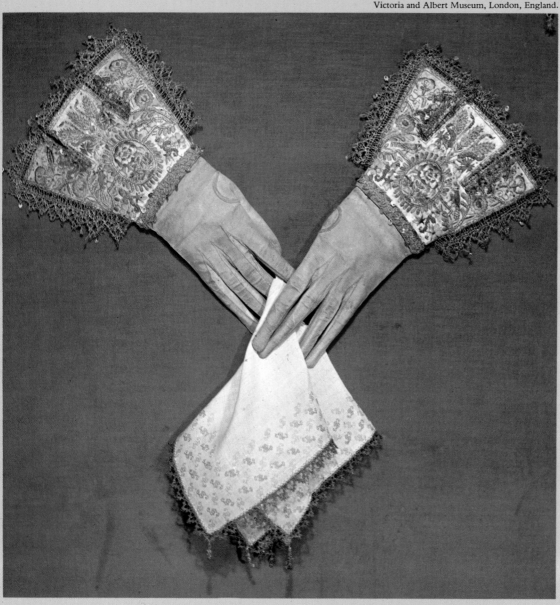

Collector's Piece

Gloves fit for a Queen

At the court of Queen Elizabeth 1, the practice of giving presents at New Year was an important part of court life, and embroidery was considered a valuable gift, worthy of being presented to the Queen. Elizabeth received presents from all her high-ranking officials—embroidered gowns, petticoats, doublets and other articles of clothing—and embroidered gloves featured high on the list. The Queen was presented

with costly embroidered gloves on other occasions also; she received a pair from both Oxford and Cambridge Universities when she visited them. The embroidered gloves of this period were so ornate and heavy that they were no longer regarded as useful articles but purely as ornamentation. They were rarely worn, and subsequently examples of the beautiful work have survived, the colors only slightly faded. The gloves illustrated are made of pale colored

doeskin with gauntlets of silk cut into six scallops or tabs. The crimson velvet "mittens" have their gauntlets cut into eight tabs. The designs worked on both gloves are typically Elizabethan, consisting of flowers, fruits, insects and entwined stems, with each of the tabs containing a different flower or plant motif. Colored silks, gold threads and small jewels were used for the embroidery, and the doeskin gloves are trimmed with gold lace.

Old fashioned roses for modern chairs

Needle-point 28

Old fashioned flower embroidery designs make a fascinating contrast when they are used with modern furniture. This charming pattern of roses, worked in subtle colors from the chart, can be put to a wide variety of uses—chair seats, stool tops, pillows and rugs. The chart shows one complete pattern. Worked on single-mesh canvas with 14 threads to the inch, and working over two threads of canvas each way, one pattern measures approximately 16 inches by 15 inches. The rocking chair illustrated uses two complete patterns.

Yarns and stitches

Crewel wool has been used for the design and the chart is a guide to the colors of yarn used. Work the pattern in tent stitch using four strands of crewel wool.

Yarn quantities

For larger pieces of work, it is possible to work out fairly accurately how much yarn you will need. Cut a skein of crewel wool into 18 inch lengths. Divide these into groups of three or four strands (depending on the stitch you are using). Thread the group of strands into a needle and work the stitch until you reach the end of the length of yarn. Count the number of stitches you have worked and multiply this figure by the number of groups of strands in one skein. This will give you the total number of stitches which can be worked with one skein of yarn. By counting the number of stitches to be worked in that color from the chart you will be able to calculate the amount of yarn required to complete the design.

Color and yarn working chart

The colors and quantities in Appletons Crewel Wool given are for working one pattern of the design. The quantities should be doubled for working two patterns and extra background yarn can be calculated according to the instructions given in this chapter. The color key is on the left followed by the Appletons reference range and shade number, and the number of skeins required is indicated in parentheses.

Key	Code and no of skeins
	500/4 (2)
	500/3 (3)
	500/1 (1)
	800/1 (2)
	940/6 (2)
	940/5 (3)
	940/3 (2)
	991 (2)
	550/4 (1)
	550/1 (2)
	310/1 (3)
	340/5 (2)
	340/3 (2)
	430/7 (2)
	430/6 (3)
	430/8 (2)
	240/5 (2)
	900/4 (1)
	994 (2)
	860/4 (2)
	860/6 (2)
	980/5 (2)
	960/1 (2)
	960/7 (1)
	993 4 1 oz skeins

Crazy daisy craze

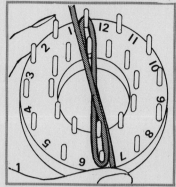

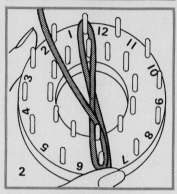

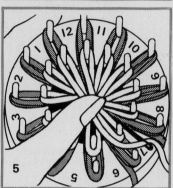

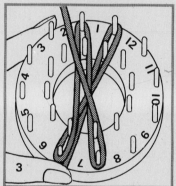

Three-dimensional daisies give an unusual effect for an afghan or bedspread. Quick and easy to do, it is great fun and is something which can be tackled by all the family.

The Multi-Fleur flower loom differs from the other looms mentioned in previous daisy work chapters. The loom consists of a plastic ring with fixed pegs set at right angles. There is an inner and an outer circle of pegs so that daisies of different sizes can be worked, or three-dimensional daisies with different sized petals. Each daisy measures about 3¼ins, and with 2oz of color A and 1oz each of colors B and C in knitting worsted weight yarn, about 32 daisies can be made working the full loom. Allowing for different gauges, each daisy takes about 4 yards color A (outer petals), 2¼ yards color B (inner petals) and 2 yards color C (joining chain).

How to wind the daisy

Work with the loom on a flat surface and space 1 at the top. Start with the large outer petals. Place the end of the yarn in space 7 and fasten with sticky tape. Take yarn across to space 1, around outer peg to space 12, back across to space 6, around outer peg to space 7 (see diagram 1). Wind yarn around same pegs twice more so that each petal has 3 loops.

Continuing with the strand at space 7, take it across to space 2 (diagram 2), around outer peg to space 1, across to space 7, around outer peg to space 8 (diagram 3). Wind yarn around same pegs twice more to complete petals.

Continue in this way in an anti-clockwise direction until all pegs have been used and there are 12 3-loop petals, ending with yarn in space 6. Cut about ½-inch of yarn beyond the loom and secure with sticky tape.

Using the B color, secure end of yarn at space 7, take it across to space 1, around inner peg to space 12, across to space 6, around inner peg to space 7. Wind yarn around same pegs once more so that each petal has 2 loops.

Continuing with yarn at space 7, take it across to space 2, around inner peg to space 1 (diagram 4), across to space 7, around inner peg to space 8. Wind yarn around same pegs once more to complete petals.

Continue in this way to wind the inner pegs until there are 12 2-loop petals, ending with yarn in space 6. Cut yarn leaving about 16 inches for sewing. Thread the end into a darning needle, pass around the inner peg to space 7 and push needle through to the back at center, taking care not to split the yarn (diagram 5). Finish off by bringing needle up through space 12, pull tightly against center back of flower, push needle through to back between strands in space 1. Continue this backstitch until every petal has a crossbar, keeping the stitch as firm and near the center as possible. End with the yarn at the back of the loom in space 10. Push

▲ *Six stages of winding a daisy on to the Multi-Fleur loom*

the needle through from back to front at center and then from front to back at inner edge of any backstitch (diagram 6). Gently remove flower from loom and fasten the end securely on the wrong side. Trim the loose ends close to the center of the flower.

Joining the daisies

With the method of joining illustrated (see diagram) the daisies retain their circular shape rather than making them into squares (Daisy work chapter 3, page 554) or joining in each daisy as it is worked (Daisy work chapter 2, page 214). This is an ideal method for a wide variety of pretty things. Begin with a small project such as a baby's bonnet or a pretty evening shawl with matching handbag.

1st row With crochet hook No.F (4.00 mm) and color C, make loop on hook. Working from right side of flower, work 1sc in any outer petal of a flower, taking all 3 loops with care not to twist them. * Ch5, 1sc in next petal, repeat from * 6 times more, leaving last 4 petals free. ***Skipping 5ch, work 1sc in any petal on a new flower, ch5, 1sc in next petal on new flower, drop loop from hook, insert hook in sc of 7th petal of previous flower and then in dropped loop of new flower, draw this loop through sc. ** Ch5, 1sc in next petal of new flower, repeat from ** 5 times more, leaving last 4 petals free. Repeat from *** as desired.

Continue across free petals of first row as follows: from right side ch5, 1sc in 9th petal of last flower, * ch5, 1sc in next petal, repeat

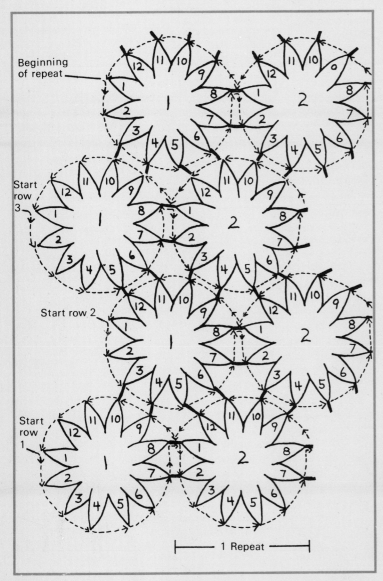

▲ Follow the arrows on this chart for the method of joining the daisies

▲ Detail of the daisy afghan shown here as a bedspread

from * twice more. *** Ch5, 1sc in joining between last and next flower, ch5, 1sc in 9th petal of next flower, ** ch5, 1sc in next petal, repeat from ** twice more. Repeat from *** across all free petals ending with ch5, join with a ss into first sc. Fasten off.

NB Rows are always worked from left to right.

2nd row 1sc in any petal of a new flower, ch5, 1sc in 2nd petal, ch5, 1sc in 3rd petal, drop loop from hook, insert hook in sc on 10th petal of first flower of previous row and then in dropped loop, draw this loop through sc, ch5, 1sc in 4th petal of new flower, join to next petal of first flower of previous row as before, ch5, 1sc in 5th petal of new flower, join to 12th petal of 2nd flower of previous row, ch5, 1sc in 6th petal of new flower, join to sc on next petal of 2nd flower of previous row, ch5, 1sc in 7th petal of new flower, ch5, 1sc in 8th petal of new flower, leaving last 4 petals free. ***Skipping 5ch, work 1sc in any petal of a new flower, ch5, 1sc in 2nd petal of new flower, join to 7th petal of last flower, ch5, 1sc in 3rd petal of new flower, join to next free petal in previous row, ch5, 1sc in 4th petal of new flower, join to next free petal in previous row, ch5, 1sc in 5th petal of new flower, join to next free petal of next flower in previous row, ch5, 1sc in 6th petal of new flower, join to next free petal in previous row, ch5, 1sc in 7th petal of new flower, ch5, 1sc in 8th petal of new flower leaving last 4 petals free. Repeat from *** as desired. Continue across free petals as for 1st row.

3rd row 1sc in any petal of a new flower, * ch5, 1sc in next petal, repeat from * 3 times more, join to sc on 12th petal of first flower of previous row, ch5, 1sc in 6th petal of new flower, join to next petal in previous row, ch5, 1sc in 7th petal of new flower, ch5, 1sc in 8th petal of new flower, leaving last 4 petals free. Repeat from 2nd row *** to second last flower, skipping 5ch, work 1sc in any petal of a new flower, ch5, 1sc in 2nd petal of new flower, join to 7th petal of last flower, ch5, 1sc in 3rd petal of new flower, join to next free petal in previous row, ch5, 1sc in 4th petal of new flower, join to next free petal in previous row, * ch5, 1sc in next petal of new flower, repeat from * 3 times more, ending with sc in 8th petal, leaving last 4 petals free. Continue across free petals as given for 1st row.

Repeat 2nd and 3rd rows as desired.

Fasten ends securely.

To make an afghan

An afghan can be used as a coverlet or a bedspread. To make one measuring about 48in by 62in you will need 357 daisies. This will take 18oz color A (illustrated here in white), 10oz color B (yellow) and 8oz color C (green), all in knitting worsted. Join the daisies in alternating rows of 16 and 15 to make 23 rows in all. When completed, pin out with rust proof pins and cover with a damp cloth. Do not remove pins until cloth is dry.

All kinds of fastenings in dressmaking

The tone of a garment, casual or formal, is often set by the kind of fastening used on it, and in many cases a fastening may be the only fashion detail on a garment.

Fastenings can be functional, in which case they have to be very firmly and carefully constructed, or they can be purely decorative, as in the case of a simulated buttoned tab. Sometimes, however, a fastening can be both functional and decorative and a perfect example of this is a dress with a Center Front opening fastened from neck to hem with rouleau loops. A functional fastening in quite a different mood is the fly fastening, shown on the opposite page. This is a Vogue Paris original Pattern.

Previous chapters have dealt with some buttoned and tab Center Front fastenings, also rouleau loop and tie fastenings, and have shown the methods of constructing these so that you can apply them to any garment you wish. This chapter gives several more types of fastenings, including fly and rouleau loop cluster fastenings, to provide you with further ideas for completely changing the mood of your favorite styles.

Fabrics and fastenings

The fastening on a garment should be very carefully planned as it must not only suit the style of the garment but also the fabric it is made from. The basic construction must be correct if the fastening is to retain its shape for the lifetime of the garment, and also to insure that it does not break down and so make the garment look worn out before its time.

The weight of the fabric used is the deciding factor, and a lot of dressmaking experience is required to make the right decision.

On bulky fabrics the position of the fastening is also important, especially if you have certain figure problems.

Fastenings should always remain flat and not rise from the surface of the garment in a high ridge. If this happens it could be the result of faulty construction.

Fly fastenings

Fly fastenings are concealed fastenings used when it is necessary for the surface of a garment to retain an uncluttered look and when the cut of the garment is more important than the detail. They are mostly worked into a seamline, such as a Center Front seam or panel seam.

Although fly fastenings are often closed with a zipper, the traditional way to close them is with buttonholes set into a button bar attached to the underside of the right front.

For demonstrating the fly fastenings a dress with a Center Front seam and no waist seam has been used.

Buttoned fly fastening

The pattern. You will need pattern pieces for a right Front, left Front, right front facing, left front facing, back neck facing, Back. Use a right Front pattern without wrap (figure **1**).

Make a right front facing 2 inches wide at the shoulder edge and 3 inches wide down the front, the shape of the front and neck edges as shown (figure **1**).

For the left Front add $1\frac{1}{2}$ inches to the Center Front edge for a wrap (figure **2**), then make a left front facing 2 inches wide at the shoulder edge and 3 inches wide down the front.

Make a back neck facing 2 inches wide (figure **3**).

Lining. Both right Front edge and right front facing need to be lined.

Make a lining pattern 2 inches wide, as in figure **4**, and use this pattern to cut the lining for both.

Cutting out. Cut facing and lining pieces with seam allowance all around.

Making up. To avoid showing seam edges at the neck edge of the fly fastening, start the buttoning $2\frac{1}{2}$ inches down from the neckline. Line the right Front and right front facing as shown (figure **5**).

To do this, place the lining and fabric together, right sides facing and Center Fronts coinciding, and stitch the Center Front starting $2\frac{1}{2}$ inches down from the neck edge. Snip the seam allowance at the top of the stitching and turn the lining to the inside.

Working on the facing, baste and press the lining to the inside of the facing and make a row of vertical buttonholes $\frac{3}{4}$ inches from the Center Front edge to fit $\frac{5}{8}$ inch diameter flat buttons.

Join the right and left front facings to the back neck facing at the shoulder seams.

Place the joined facing to the garment right sides together. Starting at the snipped seam allowance on the right Front, stitch the facing in place up to the neck edge, around the neck and down the left Front.

Turn the facing into the garment, pin in place and edge-baste.

Pin the buttonholed section of the facing to the garment a fraction inside the front edge so the facing will not show. Baste it firmly. Measure in $1\frac{1}{2}$ inches from the edge of the right Front and topstitch as shown (figure **6**), catching in all layers of fabric.

Fasten the neck edge with a snap fastener or reversed button and buttonhole (figure **7**), and sew on the other buttons.

Zipper fly fastening

The pattern. You will need patterns for a Back, right Front, left Front, right front facing, left front neck facing, back neck facing. Make right Front, right front facing and back neck facing patterns as for the buttoned fly fastening (see figures **1** and **3**).

Make a left Front pattern as in figure **8**, adding $\frac{1}{2}$ inch to the Center Front edge, also make a left front neck facing as shown.

Cutting out. Cut all edges with seam allowances.

Making up. Complete the garment first. Stitch the right front, back neck and left front neck facings at shoulders. Place on garment, right sides together. Starting at the bottom of the fastening on the right Front, stitch up to the neck and around the neck.

Fold under the seam allowance on the left Front along the zipper stitching line, then pin and baste the folded edge close to the zipper teeth. Stitch firmly in place (figure **9**).

Fold the faced right Front edge over the zipper so that the Center Front lines meet (figure **10a**) and baste down firmly.

Topstitch the zipper in place on the right Front working on the right side of the fabric, catching in all layers of fabric plus zipper tape. If the opening is in a seam which continues below the fastening, finish the lower end of the topstitching with a half miter.

Snip into the seam allowance on the left Front as shown (figure **10b**). Fold the neck facing on the left Front opening over the zipper tape and hand-sew in place. Fasten the top with a hook and eye.

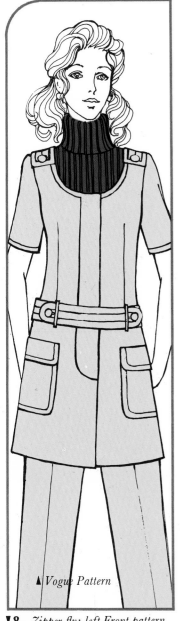

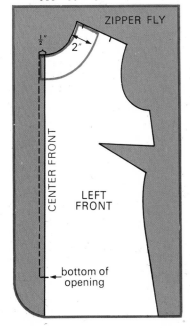

▲ *Vogue Pattern*

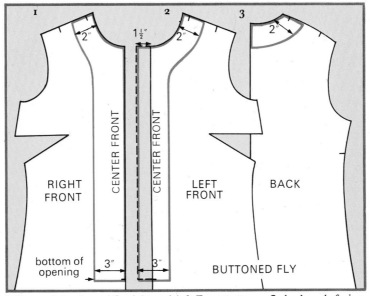

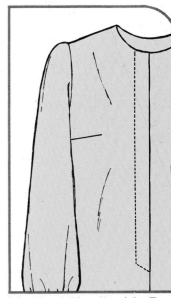

▲ *Buttoned fly:* **1.** *and* **2.** *right and left Front patterns;* **3.** *back neck facing*
▼ *Buttoned fly:* **4.** *Lining pattern;* **5.** *The lined right Front and facing*

▲ **6.** *Topstitching the right Front*
▼ **7.** *Reversed button and buttonhole*

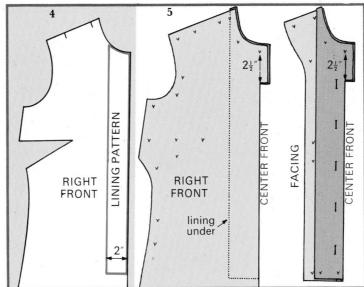

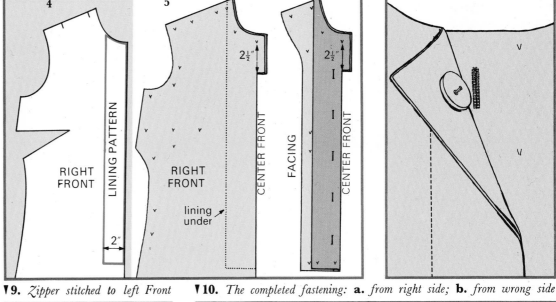

▼ **8.** *Zipper fly: left Front pattern*

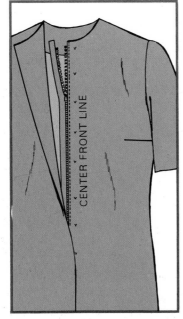

▼ **9.** *Zipper stitched to left Front*

▼ **10.** *The completed fastening:* **a.** *from right side;* **b.** *from wrong side*

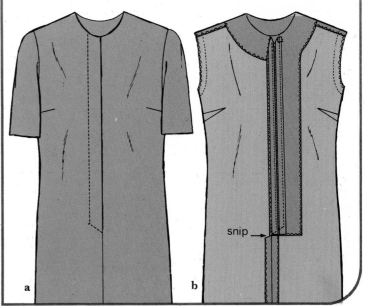

Loops, buckles and bows

These are weak fastenings, so if they are likely to be submitted to occasional strain, such as at a waistline, always make a concealed hook and eye fastening at that point.

Looped fastening

Apart from the conventional placing of rouleau loops, an attractive couture idea is to make a cluster of loops and space them out evenly along a front bodice opening (figure **11a**).

Stitch two loops closely together then make a third forming the shape of a clover leaf (figure **11b**).

Since the center loop ends are longer, stitch the rouleaux together until there is only enough space left to allow the button to go through (figure **11c**).

Bow fastening

Where a fastening is closed with one button only it is often difficult to give it the right importance unless a single, really outstanding button can be found.

But all too often the search for a button in the right size, shape and color is fruitless. A bow of soft leather, or any other material, can make an attractive alternative (figure **12a**).

Following the illustrations, cut and make a pattern for a bow with splaying ends (figure **12b**). Make four vertical buttonholes $\frac{3}{4}$ inch long, two on the right side and two on the left (figure **12c**). Slip the bow through the buttonholes and tie.

Buckled fastenings

An attractive alternative to a buttoned fastening, such as that illustrated here, can be achieved with a buckle (figure **13a**). To make the tab cut the right end of the yoke front 4 inches longer, splaying it out so that it is a little wider at the end. Attach a buckle, slightly smaller than the tab, to the left side and slot the end of the right yoke through it.

The diagonal seamline of a cross-over garment can be given detail by stitching tab ends into the seam and slotting the tabs through pretty matching buckles (figure **13b**).

Buckled fastenings need not have a sporty appearance. A silver or diamanté buckle can be used to good effect on a cocktail dress, adding an individual finishing touch.

Frogs

Frogs are a very easy method of decorating a garment.

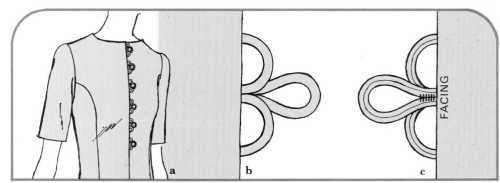

▲ **11a.** *The rouleau loop cluster along front bodice opening:* **b.** *from right side;* **c.** *from wrong side*

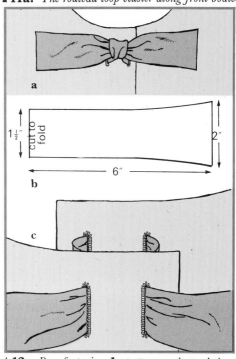

▲ **12a.** *Bow fastening;* **b.** *pattern;* **c.** *buttonholes*

▲ **13.** *Buckles on:* **a.** *yoke;* **b.** *diagonal seam*

Frogs can be made in rouleau, cord or braid.

When made from rouleau or cord the frogs are generally worked separately (figures **14a** and **b**) and then attached to the garment with small slip stitches. The button is also incorporated in the frog so that it can be used as an edge to edge fastening (figure **14c**).

When working with stitched rouleau make sure that the seam does not lie on top of the finished frog.

Using braid, the frog is usually worked straight onto the garment.

If you are matching opposites, make sure that the cord or rouleau goes over and under at the same places, but in reverse.

Tuck the ends of the cord carefully under the frog so that they can be stitched out of sight, and make sure they do not form a thickness which will lift the frog when it is stitched on the garment.

Simple frogs can be worked free hand by using the finger to gauge the size of the loops. More complicated designs, however, are usually worked over a drawn up pattern, carefully pinned and then stitched together.

Buttons

All dressmakers know how the appearance of a dress changes when the buttons are sewn on. It is often just the buttons used which turn the fastening into something special.

The type of button you choose decides the number to use. If you want lots of buttons keep them plain so that the whole fastening shows up as cleverly planned detail. Important looking buttons should never be crowded even if they are small.

Thick buttons will always create a three dimensional effect and add to the impression of bulk, so use them sparingly. Choose either very large buttons or very small ones, and avoid in-between sizes.

Many buttons which do not look good on vertical fastenings can be used successfully on a diagonal fastening, which has a diminishing effect.

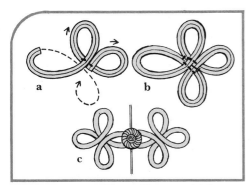

▲ **14.** *Frogs:* **a.** *and* **b.** *making;* **c.** *with button*

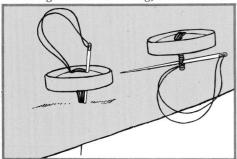

▲ **16.** *Making a thread shank*

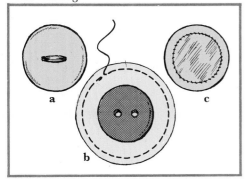

▲ **18a.** *Covered button;* **b.** *covering;* **c.** *lining*

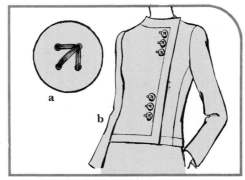

▲ **15a.** *Button with arrowheads:* **b.** *attractive group*

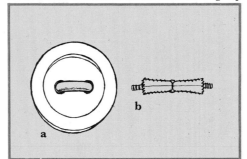

▲ **17a.** *Rouleau shank;* **b.** *from wrong side*

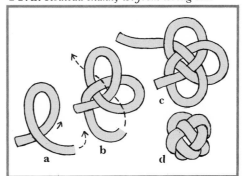

▲ **19.** *Steps in making a Chinese ball button*

Ordinary fastenings are turned into something special when you stitch on a button attractively. Figure **15a** shows a four drill button stitched on in the shape of an arrowhead, which can be emphasized with shiny silk thread. Part of the attraction can be achieved by the arrangement of buttons in groups (figure **15b**).

The crossover method of stitching on buttons is only used on men's trouser buttons or on that type of button which has a sunken center. If a cross-stitch is used on a flat centered button the thread soon shows signs of wear and it often becomes shiny and discolored.

About button shanks

The length of a button shank should correspond to the thickness of the button-hole.

Buttons with a built-in shank don't need the addition of a thread shank.

Buttons without a shank and with horizontal holes drilled into the underside are only intended for decoration, to be stitched on the surface of a garment. Making a

thread shank on this type of button will only result in sprawling and unsightly stitches.

To make a thread shank follow the steps in figure **16.**

The type of button to avoid altogether is one with a shank so wide that it makes the buttonhole gape when it fits around it. A thread shank here is not the answer either, as the shank and button will sit on top of the buttonhole and reveal the underside of the button.

When using buttons with small metal loop shanks for decorative purposes make an eyelet into the fabric and draw the shank to the inside of the garment. This will keep the button from tilting.

Rouleau button shank

Buttons with large drill holes can be stitched on with a fine rouleau (figure **17a**). Make a rouleau $\frac{1}{8}$ inch wide. Cut off a piece about $1\frac{1}{4}$ inches long and fill with buttonhole gimp (this is a cord-like thread mainly used by tailors). Then thread through the drill holes.

To attach the button, prize the weave of the garment open with a stiletto or the pointed end of a No.4 knitting needle, without breaking the threads of the fabric. Work the hole through the interfacing as well.

Push the ends of the rouleau through the hole to the underside. Leave enough rouleau between the button and the garment to make a shank and stitch the ends of the rouleau to the interfacing, spreading them quite flat and catching the ends of the gimp into the stitches so it cannot work out (figure **17b**). The gimp will keep the rouleau from stretching and making the button loose.

In hard weaves it may be necessary to make an eyelet through which to take the rouleau. It is then sewn on as before.

Fabric covered buttons

Fabric covered buttons should only be used with bound buttonholes, as the friction of a hand-made buttonhole will soon wear away the fabric of a covered button.

Just as there are wrong fabrics for bound buttonholes, there are wrong fabrics for covered buttons. Avoid stiff fabrics as they usually form points around the edges unless they are molded by machine.

A loose woven fabric used to cover buttons should first be lined.

Covering a button

Here is a quick way to cover buttons to match a garment (figure **18a**).

You can use odd buttons for this but make sure they are all the same shape on the underside first.

Cut a circle a little larger than the size of the button and sew a row of running stitches close to the edge. Place the button in the center and draw up the fullness (figure **18b**). Fasten off the stitches firmly underneath and line the underside with another circle of matching fabric (figure **18c**).

Stitch on the button with shiny matching silk using the drill holes.

Chinese ball button

This type of button is only used for decorative purposes as it will collapse if subjected to strain.

These buttons are made from cord, rouleau or braid, folded as shown (figure **19**).

To retain a good rounded shape when the button is sewn to the garment, make one knot from the ends, cut them off short and stitch them out of sight.

1299

Fashion Flair

Flowery pillows

These two flower motifs can be used in a variety of arrangements to create pleasing designs for pillows, embroidered in wool or floss, or in a combination of appliqué and embroidery.

1. *A diagonal row of motifs with one motif placed in each opposite corner.*
2. *Motifs arranged as an all-over pattern.*
3. *Flower motifs in spaced diagonal lines for an attractive all-over pattern.*
4. *Motifs set in horizontal lines for a formal style.*
5. *Motifs grouped into a square central design.*
6. *An alternative square arrangement for a round pillow.*
7. *Motifs arranged as a bold border around the edge of the pillow.*

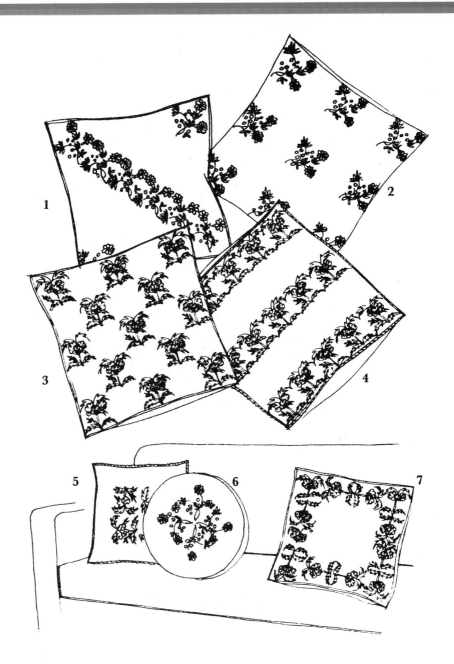

Pattern Library

Apple blossom appliqué

This simple spray of apple blossoms makes a charming design for appliqué work. Trace the lifesize design from this page or enlarge it. Lawn in clear, bright colors has been applied with pin stitch and the details on petals and leaves are worked in outline stitch. The flower centers are decorated with French knots. Work several rows of outline stitch for the stem.

Guardsman pajama case

Knit this Guardsman to protect your pajamas!

Size
Height about 22½in.
Height of body about 14in.

> **Gauge**
> 7 sts and 9 rows to 1in
> over st st worked on
> No.3 needles.

Materials
Sports yarn
1 (2oz) skein cream,
3 skeins black, 1 skein red,
1 skein white, 1 skein yellow
One pair No.3 needles
(or Canadian No.10)
One pair No.6 needles
(or Canadian No.7)
One No.C (2.50 mm)
crochet hook
One small stitch holder
3 small gold buttons
One small gold buckle
One 6in zipper
Filling

Body

Right leg
Using No.3 needles and
cream, cast on 14 sts.
Work in st st beg with K row.
Inc one st at each end of 1st
and 2nd rows.
Work 4 rows.*
7th row K to last 2 sts, K2 tog.
8th row Bind off 2 sts, P to
end.
Rep 7th and 8th rows once.
**Work 4 rows.
Inc one st at beg of next and
every 4th row until 17 sts rem.
Work 3 rows.**
Slip sts on holder.

Left leg
Work as given for right leg
to *
Next row Bind off 2 sts, K to
end.

1302

Next row P to last 2 sts, P2
tog.
Rep last 2 rows once more.
Work as for right leg from **
to ** reversing shaping.

Join legs for body
With RS facing, K across sts
from left leg, then K across sts
from holder. 34 sts.
Work 3 rows.
Next row *K1, K2 tog tbl,
K11, K2 tog, K1, rep from *
once more.
Work 3 rows.
Next row *K1, K2 tog tbl,
K9, K2 tog, K1, rep from *
once more.
Work 3 rows.
Next row *K1, K2 tog tbl,
K7, K2 tog, K1, rep from *
once more.
Work 3 rows.
Next row *K1, K2 tog tbl,
K5, K2 tog, K1, rep from *
once more.
Work 7 rows.
Inc one st at each end of next
and every 4th row until there
are 24 sts.
Work 3 rows. Bind off.
Work another piece in same
manner. Seam together RS
facing except at center neck
edge. Turn out and stuff.

Arms

Using No.3 needles and
cream, cast on 9 sts.
1st row Inc in first st, K2,
inc in each of next 2 sts, K2,
inc in next st, K1.
2nd row Inc in first st, P4,
inc in each of next 2 sts, P4,
inc in next st, P1.
Work 8 rows.
Inc one st at each end of next
row.
Work 15 rows more. Bind off.

Work 2nd arm in same manner.
Fold each arm in half and
seam except for bound-off
edge. Stuff lightly and seam
remaining edge. Sew to sides
of body below shoulders.

Head

Using No.3 needles and
cream, cast on 20 sts.
Work in st st beg with a K
row. Work 2 rows.
3rd row K1, *K up 1 tbl,
K1, rep from * to end.
Work 3 rows.
7th row K1, *K up 1 tbl, K2,
rep from * to end.
Work 3 rows.
11th row K1, *K up 1 tbl,
K3, rep from * to end.
Work 19 rows.
1st dec row K1, *K2 tog,
K2, rep from * to end.
Work 3 rows.
2nd dec row K1, *K2 tog,
K1, rep from * to end.
Work 3 rows.
3rd dec row K1, *K2 tog,
rep from * to end.
Work 2 rows. Bind off.
Seam sides and stuff. Sew
bound-off edge to body.

Trousers

Using No.3 needles and
black, cast on 8 sts for boot.
Work in st st beg with K row.
Work 20 rows.
21st row Cast on 14 sts, K to
end.
22nd row Cast on 14 sts, P
all sts. 36 sts.
Work 6 rows. Break off black.
With RS facing, slip first 14
sts onto right-hand needle.
Join white to next st and K7,
K2 tog, turn. Work on these
sts for foot top.
Next row P7, P2 tog. Turn.
Rep last 2 rows 3 times more.
Next row K across center sts
and 10 sts at left side.
Next row P across all 28 sts.
Work 4 rows.
Inc one st at each end of next
and following 4th row.
P 1 row. Break off white.
Attach black and work 2 rows.
Inc one st at each end of next
and every following 4th row
until there are 40 sts.
P 1 row. Slip sts on holder.
Work 2nd leg in same manner.

Join for body
1st row K across sts from last
leg worked then across sts of
first leg from holder. 80 sts.
P 1 row.
3rd row *K1, K2 tog tbl,
K34, K2 tog, K1, rep from *
once more.
P 1 row.
5th row *K1, K2 tog tbl,
K32, K2 tog, K1, rep from *
once more.
P 1 row.
7th row *K1, K2 tog tbl,
K30, K2 tog, K1, rep from *
once more.
P 1 row.
9th row *K1, K2 tog tbl,
K28, K2 tog, K1, rep from *
once more.
Work 3 rows.
13th row *K1, K2 tog tbl,
K26, K2 tog, K1, rep from *
once more.
Work 3 rows.
17th row *K1, K2 tog tbl,
K24, K2 tog, K1, rep from *
once more.
Work 1 row.
Work 4 rows in K1, P1 rib.
Bind off in rib.

Jacket sleeves

Using No.3 needles and red,
cast on 20 sts.
K 4 rows.
Change to st st beg with a K
row.
Work 2 rows.
Inc one st at each end of next
and every following 4th row
until there are 28 sts.
P 1 row.

Shape cap
Last row Bind off 2 sts at
each end of row. Slip sts on
holder.
Work second sleeve in same
manner.

Jacket

Using No.3 needles and red,
cast on 70 sts. K 4 rows.
5th row K.
6th row K2, P to last 2 sts,
K2.
Rep 5th and 6th rows twice.
1st dec row K16, K2 tog,
K14, K2 tog, K2, K2 tog,
K14, K2 tog, K16.
Work 3 rows.
2nd dec row K15, K2 tog,

K13, K2 tog, K2, K2 tog,
K13, K2 tog, K15.
Work 3 rows.
3rd dec row K14, K2 tog,
K12, K2 tog, K2, K2 tog,
K12, K2 tog, K14.
Next row K2, P1, yrn, P2
tog, P to last 2 sts, K2.
Work 2 rows.
4th dec row K13, K2 tog,
K11, K2 tog, K2, K2 tog,
K11, K2 tog, K13.
Work 3 rows.
Next row K13, bind off
5 sts, K to last 18 sts, bind off
5 sts, K13.

Join sleeves and body
1st row K2, P1, yrn, P2 tog,
P9, P across sts from first
sleeve, P across sts for Back,
P across sts from second
sleeve, P to last 2 sts of Front,
K2.
2nd row K11, K2 tog twice,
K20, K2 tog twice, K14, K2
tog twice, K20, K2 tog twice,
K11.
3rd row K2, P to last 2 sts,
K2.
4th row K10, K2 tog twice,
K18, K2 tog twice, K12, K2
tog twice, K18, K2 tog twice,
K10.
5th row K2, P to last 2 sts,
K2.
6th row K9, K2 tog 3 times,
K12, K2 tog 3 times, K10,
K2 tog 3 times, K12, K2 tog
3 times, K9.
7th row K2, P to last 2 sts,
K2.
8th row K8, *K2 tog 3 times,
K8, rep from * 3 times more.
9th row K2, P1, yrn, P2 tog,
P to last 2 sts, K2.
10th row Bind off 2 sts, K to
end.
11th row Bind off 2 sts, *P1,
P2 tog, rep from * to last 2
sts, P2.
K4 rows for collar. Bind off.
Seam sleeves and underarm.

Gloves

Using No.3 needles and
white, cast on 20 sts.
Work in st st beg with a K
row.
Work 6 rows.
1st dec row *K2 tog, K6,
K2 tog, rep from * once.
P 1 row.
2nd dec row *K2 tog, K4,

K2 tog, rep from * once more.
P 1 row.
3rd dec row *K2 tog, K2,
K2 tog, rep from * once more.
P 1 row.
4th dec row *K2 tog, rep
from * to end.
Thread yarn through rem sts
and draw up.
Seam side of glove. Sew
inside of jacket sleeves.

Belt

Using No.C crochet hook
and white, ch62.
Work 2 rows sc.
Sew buckle to one end.

Epaulettes

Using No.C crochet hook
and yellow, ch8.
1st row 1sc in 2nd ch from
hook, 1sc in each of next 2ch,
ss into next ch. Turn.
2nd row Ch1, 1sc in each of
next 2sc, 2sc in next sc, 5sc
in end turning to work along
other side of ch, 2sc in next
ch, 1sc in each of next 2ch,
ss into next ch.

Fringe
Cut lengths of yellow 3½in
long. Fold 2 strands in half
and draw through edge st of
epaulette with No.C hook.
Pass ends through loop and
pull tight. Continue in this
manner around epaulette
edges. Sew to top of jacket.

Frog trim

Using black, embroider
frogs across Fronts and
around buttonholes.

Bear's skin

Using No.6 needles and black
yarn double, cast on 19 sts.
1st row K.
2nd row K1, *insert needle
into next st as if to K, wind
yarn twice around needle point
and 2 fingers of left hand,
then around needle point
only, draw through loops and
return to left-hand needle, K
loops and original st tog tbl —
called ML—, K1, rep from *
to end.
Rep last 2 rows inc one st at

▲ *A guardsman's zippered bear's skin to conceal your nightgown*

each end of 9th and every
following 10th row until work
measures 12in. Bind off.
Make a second piece.
Seam sides. Stitch cast-on
edge around head. Sew fastener
to bound-off edge or leave
open. Make a chain in double
yarn for chin strap. Sew to
either side around face.

Moustache

Cut 30 6in strands of black.
Tie center and stitch to face.

Finishing

DO NOT PRESS.
Sew on felt eyes.
Sew on buttons to jacket.

Classic ribbed sweater

This useful pullover, knitted in a soft yet hard-wearing yarn, will make an indispensable addition to a boy's wardrobe. The comfortable saddle top shoulders allow complete freedom of movement, and the wide rib adds individuality to this plain classic.

Sizes

Directions are for 28in chest. The figures in brackets [ ] refer to the 30 and 32in sizes respectively.
Length at center back, 17½ [18¾:20]in.
Sleeve seam, 13½[14½:16]in.

Gauge

6½ sts and 8½ rows to 1in over pattern worked on No.3 needles.

Materials

Sports yarn
8[8:9] (2oz) skeins
One pair No.2 nèedles
 (or Canadian No.11)
One pair No.3 needles
 (or Canadian No.10)
One large stitch holder

Back

Using No.2 needles, cast on 100[108:116] sts.
1st row K1, P2, *K2, P2, rep from * to last st, K1.
2nd row P1, K2, *P2, K2, rep from * to last st, P1.
Rep 1st and 2nd rows 9 times more.
Change to No.3 needles and rib patt.
1st row K4[8:2] sts, P2, *K8, P2, rep from * to last 4[8:2] sts, K to end.

2nd row P4[8:2] sts, K2, *P8, K2, rep from * to last 4[8:2] sts, P to end.
These 2 rows form wide rib patt.
Continue in patt until work measures 11½[12½:13½]in or desired length to underarm, ending with a WS row.

Shape armholes

Bind off 3[4:5] sts at beg of next 2 rows.
Bind off one st at beg of next 6[8:10] rows.
Work without shaping until armholes measure 6[6¼:6½]in, ending with a WS row.

Shape shoulders

Bind off at beg of next and every row 7 sts 0[2:4] times and 6 sts 10[8:6] times.
Slip rem 28[30:32] sts on holder for neckband.

Front

Work as given for Back until armholes measure same length to shoulder. End with WS row.

Shape neck and shoulders

1st row Bind off 6[7:7] sts, patt 31[31:32] sts. Turn. 32 [32:33] sts on needle.
2nd row Bind off 2 sts, patt to end.
3rd row Bind off 6[6:7] sts, patt to last 2 sts, K2 tog.
4th row K2 tog, patt to end.
5th row Bind off 6 sts, patt to last 2 sts, K2 tog.
6th row K2 tog, patt to end.
Rep 5th and 6th rows once more.
Bind off rem 6 sts.
With RS of work facing, slip center 12[14:14] sts onto holder, attach yarn to rem 38[39:40] sts for right shoulder, patt to end.

2nd row Bind off 6[7:7] sts, patt to end.
3rd row Bind off 2 sts, patt to end.
4th row Bind off 6[6:7] sts, patt to last 2 sts, K2 tog.
5th row K2 tog, patt to end.
6th row Bind off 6 sts, patt to last 2 sts, K2 tog.
7th row K2 tog, patt to end.
Rep 6th and 7th rows once more.
Bind off rem 6 sts.

Right sleeve

Using No.2 needles, cast on 52[56:60] sts.
Work in K2, P2 rib as given for Back for 26 rows.
Change to No.3 needles.
1st row K0[2:4] sts, P2, *K8, P2, rep from * to last 0[2:4] sts, K to end.
2nd row P0[2:4] sts, K2, *P8, K2, rep from * to last 0[2:4] sts, P to end.
Continue in patt, inc one st at each end of 3rd and every 6th row until there are 80[84:88] sts.
Continue without shaping until sleeve measures 13½ [14½:16]in, or desired underarm length, ending with a WS row.

Shape cap

Bind off 3[4:5] sts at beg of next 2 rows.
Bind off 2 sts at beg of next 4 rows.
Dec one st at beg of next 18[20:22] rows.
Bind off 2 sts at beg of next 14 rows.
Dec one st at beg of next 2 rows.**
Work 35[35:37] rows on rem 18 sts, ending with a WS row.

Shape neck edge

At neck edge, bind off 6 sts; 3 sts every other row twice; then 2 sts every other row 3 times.

Left sleeve

Work as given for Right sleeve to **.
Work 36[36:38] rows on rem 18 sts, ending with a RS row.

Shape neck edge

Work as given for Right sleeve.

▼*Close-up detail of the neckline and the saddle shoulders*

Neckband

Sew top of Left sleeve to Front and Back left shoulder. Sew top of Right sleeve to Front right shoulder.

Using No.2 needles, K across 28[30:32] sts from Back neck holder, pick up and K20 sts from sleeve cap, pick up and K12 sts down left side of front neck, K12[14:16] sts from Front neck holder, pick up and K12 sts up right side of neck and pick up and K20 sts from other sleeve cap. 104[108:112] sts.

1st row *K2, P2, rep from * to end.

Rep 1st row 11 times more. Bind off. Use invisible binding-off method for the best finish. To bind off invisibly:

1st row *K1, ytf, sl 1, ytb, rep from * to end.

Rep 1st row 3 times more. Break yarn leaving an end at least three times the length of the completed neck edge. Thread end into a darning needle and work stitches as follows—insert needle into first K st as if to P, draw yarn through leaving st on needle, *insert needle knitwise into first K st and draw yarn through slipping st off the left-hand needle, pass over the P st and insert needle into next K st purlwise, draw yarn through and leave st on needle, insert needle purlwise into first P st, draw yarn through and slip off needle, pass needle behind K st and insert needle knitwise into next P st, draw yarn through leaving st on needle, rep from * working into 2 K sts and 2 P sts alternately until all stitches are worked off. Darn in end of thread to fasten off.

Finishing

Sew Back shoulder to top of Right sleeve. Sew sleeves into armholes. Join side and sleeve seams.

Press lightly under a damp cloth with a cool iron.

◄ *Hardwearing and masculine enough for any boy*

Elegant handbag in crochet

Size
Width, 9½in.
Depth, 10in.
Gusset, 10in by 4½in.

Gauge
One patt rep measures ⅞in worked with No.10 steel crochet hook

Materials
Clark's Big Ball Mercerized Cotton No.30
4 (350yd) balls
One No.10 (1.00 mm) steel crochet hook
One 9in handbag frame
½yd 36in wide fabric for backing
½yd 36in wide lining fabric
½yd bonded interlining 32in wide
Piece of cardboard for base 9½in by 4½in

Main section

Ch324. Join with a ss to form a ring, making sure that it does not twist.

1st round Ch3, 1dc in each ch, join with a ss into 3rd of 3ch.

2nd round Ch3, *5dc in next dc, remove loop from hook, insert hook in first of 5dc and draw through dropped loop, ch1,—called 1pc st (popcorn stitch)—, ch1, skip 1dc, 1pc st in next dc, 1dc in next dc, ch2, skip 2dc, 1dc in each of next 2dc, 1pc st in next dc, ch1, skip 1dc, 1dc in each of next 2dc, (ch3, skip 3dc, 1dc in each of next 2dc, ch1, skip 1dc, 1pc st in next dc, ch1, skip 1dc, 1dc in each of next 2dc) twice, ch3, skip 3dc, 1dc in each of next 2dc, ch1, skip 1dc, 1pc st in next dc, 1dc in each of

next 2dc, ch2, skip 2dc, 1dc in next dc, 1pc st in next dc, ch1, skip 1dc, 1pc st in next dc, 1dc in next dc, ch2, skip 2dc, 1dc in next dc, rep from * once more working rep in ( ) 8 times instead of twice, then rep from * once more skipping 1dc at end of rep, join with a ss into 3rd of 3ch.

3rd round Ch4, *1pc st in next sp, ch1, 1dc in next dc, ch2, skip next sp, 1dc in each of next 3 sts, 1dc in next sp, 1dc in each of next 2dc leaving last loop of each on hook, yoh and draw through all loops on hook—called joint dc made over 2 sts—, (ch5, 1 joint dc over next 2dc, 1dc in next sp, 1dc in next st, 1dc in next sp, 1 joint dc over next 2dc) twice, ch5, 1 joint dc over next 2dc, 1dc in next sp, 1dc in each of next 3 sts, 1dc in next dc, ch1, 1pc st in next sp, ch1, 1dc in next dc, ch2, 1dc in next dc, ch1, rep from * working rep in ( ) 8 times instead of twice then rep from * once more skipping 1dc and ch1 at end of rep, join with a ss into 3rd of 4ch.

4th round Ch3, *1pc st in next sp, ch1, 1pc st in next sp, 1dc in next dc, ch2, 1dc in each of next 3dc, 1 joint dc over next 2 sts, (ch3, 1dc in next sp, ch3, 1 joint dc over next 2 sts, 1dc in next dc, 1 joint dc over next 2 sts) twice, ch3, 1dc in next sp, ch3, 1 joint dc over next 2 sts, 1dc in each of next 3dc, ch2, 1dc in next dc, 1pc st in next sp, ch1, 1pc st in next sp, 1dc in next dc, ch2, 1dc in next dc, rep from * once more working rep in ( ) 8 times instead of twice, then rep

from * once more skipping 1dc at end of rep, join with a ss into 3rd of 3ch.

5th round Ch4, *1pc st in next sp, ch1, 1dc in next dc, ch2, 1dc in each of next 2dc, 1 joint dc over next 2 sts, (ch4, 1dc in next dc, ch4, skip next sp, 1 joint dc over next 3 sts) twice, ch4, 1dc in next dc, ch4, skip next sp, 1 joint dc over next 2 sts, 1dc in each of next 2dc, ch2, 1dc in next dc, ch1, 1pc st in next sp, ch1, 1dc in next dc, ch2, 1dc in next dc, ch1, rep from * once more working rep in ( ) 8 times instead of twice, then rep from * once more skipping 1dc and ch1 at end of rep, join with a ss into 3rd of 4ch.

6th round Ch3, *1pc st in next sp, ch1, 1pc st in next sp, 1dc in next dc, ch2, skip next sp, 1dc in each of next 3 sts, (ch4, 1dc in next dc, ch4, 1dc in next joint dc) 3 times, 1dc in each of next 2dc, ch2, 1dc in next dc, 1pc st in next sp, ch1, 1pc st in next sp, 1dc in next dc, ch2, 1dc in next dc, rep from * once more working rep in ( ) 9 times instead of 3 times, then rep from * once more skipping 1dc at end of rep, join with a ss into 3rd of 3ch.

7th round Ch4, *1pc st in next sp, ch1, 1dc in next dc, ch2, 1dc in each of next 3dc, (ch3, 3dc in next dc, ch3, 1dc in next dc) 3 times, 1dc in each of next 2dc, ch2, 1dc in next dc, ch1, 1pc st in next sp, ch1, 1dc in next dc, ch2, 1dc in next dc, ch1, rep from * once more working rep in ( ) 9 times instead of 3 times, then rep from * once more skipping 1dc and ch1 at end of rep, join with a ss into 3rd of 4ch.

8th round Ch3, *1pc st in next sp, ch1, 1pc st in next sp, 1dc in next dc, ch2, 1dc in each of next 3dc, (ch2, 2dc in next dc, 1dc in next dc, 2dc in next dc, ch2, 1dc in next dc) 3 times, 1dc in each of next 2dc, ch2, 1dc in next dc, 1pc st in next sp, ch1, 1pc st in next sp, 1dc in next dc, ch2, 1dc in next dc, rep from * once more working rep in ( ) 9 times instead of 3 times, then rep

from * once more skipping 1dc at end of rep, join with a ss into 3rd of 3ch.

9th round Ch4, *1pc st in next sp, ch1, 1dc in next dc, ch2, 1dc in each of next 3dc, ch1, (2dc in next dc, 1dc in each of next 3dc, 2dc in next dc, ch3, skip 1dc) twice, 2dc in next dc, 1dc in each of next 3dc, 2dc in next dc, ch1, 1dc in each of next 3dc, ch2, 1dc in next dc, ch1, 1pc st in next sp, ch1, 1dc in next dc, ch2, 1dc in next dc, ch1, rep from * working rep in ( ) 8 times instead of twice, then rep from * once more skipping 1dc and ch1 at end of rep, join with a ss into 3rd of 4ch.

10th round Ch3, *1pc st in next sp, ch1, 1pc st in next sp, 1dc in next dc, ch2, 1dc in each of next 3dc, ch1, (1dc in each of next 2dc, ch1, skip 1dc, 1pc st in next dc, ch1, skip 1dc, 1dc in each of next 2dc, ch3) twice, 1dc in each of next 2dc, ch1, skip 1dc, 1pc st in next dc, ch1, skip 1dc, 1dc in each of next 2dc, ch1, 1dc in each of next 3dc, ch2, 1dc in next dc, 1pc st in next sp, ch1, 1pc st in next sp, 1dc in next dc, ch2, 1dc in next dc, rep from * once more working rep in ( ) 8 times instead of twice, then rep from * once more skipping 1dc at end of rep, join with a ss into 3rd of 3ch.

11th round Ch4, *1pc st in next sp, ch1, 1dc in next dc, ch2, 1dc in each of next 3dc, ch2, (1 joint dc over next 2dc, 1dc in next sp, 1dc in next st, 1dc in next st, 1dc in next sp, 1 joint dc over next 2dc, ch5) twice, 1 joint dc over next 2dc, 1dc in next sp, 1dc in next st, 1dc in next sp, 1 joint dc over next 2dc, ch2, 1dc in each of next 3dc, ch2, 1dc in next dc, ch1, 1pc st in next sp, ch1, 1dc in next dc, ch2, 1dc in next dc, ch1, rep from * once more working rep in ( ) 8 times instead of twice, then rep from * once more skipping 1dc and ch1 at end of rep, join with a ss into 3rd of 4ch.

12th round Ch3, *1pc st in next sp, ch1, 1pc st in next sp, 1dc in next dc, ch2, 1dc in each of next 3dc, ch3, skip next sp, (1 joint dc over next

2 sts, 1dc in next dc, 1 joint dc over next 2 sts, ch3, 1dc in next sp, ch3) twice, 1 joint dc over next 2 sts, 1dc in next dc, 1 joint dc over next 2 sts, ch3, 1dc in each of next 3dc, ch2, 1dc in next dc, 1pc st in next sp, ch1, 1pc st in next sp, 1dc in next dc, ch2, 1dc in next dc, rep from * once more working rep in () 8 times instead of twice, then rep from * once more skipping 1dc at end of rep, join with a ss into 3rd of 3ch.

13th round Ch4, *1pc st in next sp, ch1, 1dc in next dc, ch2, 1dc in each of next 3dc, (ch4, skip next sp, 1 joint dc over next 3 sts, ch4, 1dc in next dc) 3 times, 1dc in each of next 2dc, ch2, 1dc in next dc, ch1, 1pc st in next sp, ch1, 1dc in next dc, ch2, 1dc in next dc, ch1, rep from * once more working rep in () 9 times instead of 3 times, then rep from * once more skipping 1dc and ch1 at end of rep, join with a ss into 3rd of 4ch.

14th round Ch3, *1pc st in next sp, ch1, 1pc st in next sp, 1dc in next dc, ch2, 1dc in each of next 3dc, (ch4, 1dc in next joint dc, ch4, 1dc in next dc) 3 times, 1dc in each of next 2 dc, 1dc in next dc, 1pc st in next sp, ch1, 1pc st in next sp, 1dc in next dc, ch2, 1dc in next dc, rep from * once more working rep in () 9 times instead of 3 times, then rep from * once more skipping 1dc at end of rep, join with a ss into 3rd of 3ch.

15th round Ch4, *1pc st in next sp, ch1, 1dc in next dc, ch2, 1dc in each of next 2dc, 2dc in next dc, (ch3, 1dc in next dc, ch3, 3dc in next dc) twice, ch3, 1dc in next dc, ch3, 2dc in next dc, 1dc in each of next 2 dc, 1dc in next dc, ch1, 1pc st in next sp, ch1, 1dc in next dc, ch2, 1dc in next dc, ch1, rep from * once more working rep in () 8 times instead of twice, then rep from * once more skipping 1dc and ch1 at end of rep, join with a ss into 3rd of 4ch.

16th round Ch3, *1pc st in next sp, ch1, 1pc st in next sp, 1dc in next dc, ch2, 1dc in each of next 3dc, 2dc in next dc, (ch2, 1dc in next dc, ch2, 2dc in next dc, 1dc in next dc, 2dc in next dc) twice, ch2, 1dc in next dc, ch2, 2dc in next dc, 1dc in each of next 3dc, ch2, 1dc in next dc, 1pc st in next sp, ch1, 1pc st in next sp, 1dc in next dc, ch2, 1dc in next dc, rep from * once more working rep in () 8 times instead of twice, then rep from * once more skipping 1dc at end of rep, join with a ss into 3rd of 3ch.

17th round Ch4, *1pc st in next sp, ch1, 1dc in next dc, ch2, 1dc in each of next 4dc, 2dc in next dc, (ch3, skip 1dc, 2dc in next dc, 1dc in each of next 3dc, 2dc in next dc) twice, ch3, 2dc in next dc, 1dc in each of next 4dc, ch2, 1dc in next dc, ch1, 1pc st in next sp, ch1, 1dc in next dc, ch2, 1dc in next dc, ch1, rep from * once more working rep in () 8 times instead of twice, then rep from * once more skipping 1dc and ch1 at end of rep, join with a ss into 3rd of 4ch.

18th round Ch3, *1pc st in next sp, ch1, 1pc st in next sp, 1dc in next dc, ch2, 1dc in each of next 2dc, (1pc st in next dc, ch1, skip 1dc, 1dc in each of next 2dc, ch3, 1dc in

each of next 2dc, ch1, skip 1dc) 3 times, 1pc st in next dc, 1dc in each of next 2dc, ch2, 1dc in next dc, 1pc st in next sp, ch1, 1pc st in next sp, 1dc in next dc, ch2, 1dc in next dc, rep from * once more working rep in () 9 times instead of 3 times, then rep from * once more skipping 1dc at end of rep, join with a ss into 3rd of 3ch. Rep 3rd to 18th rows twice more.

Next round Ch3, 1dc in each st, ss into 3rd of 3ch, ch1. Turn.

Top edging

1st row Ss into each of next 3dc, ch2, work 2dc in same place as last ss leaving last loop of each on hook, yoh and draw through all loops on hook—called 2dc cl—, *ch2, skip 2dc, 3dc cl in next dc, rep from * 35 times more, ch3. Turn. 36 sps.

2nd row *2dc in next sp, 1dc in next cl, rep from * ending with ch1. Turn.

3rd row 1sc in first dc, *ch2, skip 2dc, 1sc in next st, rep from * ending with ch1. Turn.

4th row 1sc in first sc, *ch2, 1pc st in last sc worked, 1sc in next sc, rep from * to end.

Fasten off.
With WS facing, attach yarn to corresponding dc on opposite side of main section, ch2, 2dc cl in same place as join, ch2, complete as before.

Base

Ch45 to measure 4½in.
1st row 1sc in 2nd ch from hook, 1sc in each ch, ch3. Turn.
2nd row (RS) Skip first sc, 1dc in each sc, ch1. Turn.
3rd row 1sc in each dc, 1sc in 3rd of 3ch, ch3. Turn. Rep last 2 rows until work measures 9½in skipping turning ch at end of last row. Fasten off.

Finishing

Dampen and pin out pieces to measurements.
Cut one piece each of backing and lining 25½in by 10½in for main section and 2 pieces each 11in by 5½in for gussets. Cut one piece of interlining 24½in by 10½in for main section and 2 pieces each 10½in by 5½in for gussets. These measurements allow ½in seam allowance on all sides except top edges of interlining.
Place interlining on wrong side of lining for main section and gussets and baste. Place two short ends of main section right sides together and pin gussets in position. Machine stitch sides and lower edge. Clip main section at corners and trim interlining close to stitching.
Omitting interlining, make another piece in the same way using backing.
Press all seams. Insert lining into backing, placing cardboard between two sections. Turn in top edge of lining over interlining. Turn in edge of backing to wrong side and slip stitch both edges together.
Sew crocheted base to crocheted main section. Insert completed lining in crocheted section and stitch in position around top edge. Attach handle.

1307

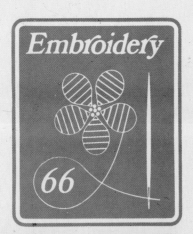

More ways with beads and sequins

This second chapter on beading deals with uses of beading for fashion garments and accessories, how to work out beading designs, and gives methods for applying designs and working out the quantities of beads and sequins required.

Beading in Fashion

Beading should be planned as an integral part of the garment design, enhancing the line, and giving the garment an added richness and an exclusive quality.

Beading for fashion must be bold enough to look effective at a distance and yet have sufficient detail for close-up interest. The arrangement of the embroidery on a garment is particularly important. Use perhaps two or three patterns on one garment. For example, a rich small scale pattern on the yoke; a small spaced spot motif over the main part of the garment, and a narrow border for edges. Dress accessories of all types can be beaded to form luxurious and exclusive fashion highlights to simple garments. One plain, well-cut dress, for example, can be turned into something special with a set of different beaded belts, collars or cuffs. A set of beaded buttons can completely transform an otherwise ordinary garment, although beaded buttons are somewhat impractical and should only be used for decoration. Beaded buckles for belts or shoes are fun to embroider, quick to make, and are ideal items for the beginner to experiment upon. Hats, headdresses, evening bags and gloves are also ideal for bead embroidery, but particular care must be taken when attaching beads to ready-made items to make sure that the tension of the stitching is firm and even.

Designs for beading

Generally, the least complicated designs are the most effective for bead embroidery. Select designs with bold shapes and avoid those formed of small shapes and thin lines as these give little scope for creating the rich, clustered textures which are possible with beading. As with all forms of embroidery, texture plays an important part and beads should be chosen in various sizes and shapes, complementing both each other and the background fabric. Many of the embroidery designs already given in Creative Hands can be adapted to bead embroidery or can be enhanced by the addition of beads. For all-over designs with a solid effect, such as those used on evening bags and belts, charted geometric designs can be used. These are worked on fine double-mesh canvas, each bead being stitched separately using a tent stitch over one set of double threads each time. For added texture, larger beads can be applied over the grounding design.

Designing directly onto fabrics

Beads lend themselves to free designing without the use of a pattern or a chart. Select beads in a color scheme to complement the fabric and mount the fabric in an embroidery frame.

Scatter the beads onto the mounted fabric and arrange them in patterns, anchoring the beads in position by pushing a pin through the hole, as the pattern develops.

Combining beading with embroidery

Beading can be combined with other forms of embroidery to great effect. Machine or hand embroidery can be used as the basis of the design, which is then highlighted and enriched with beading. For a rich and interesting effect on velvet, for example, using machine embroidery, use a thick thread, such as chenille, in the bobbin. This gives a lively texture on which to base beading. Metallic threads can also be used in the same way, or couched on by hand or with a zigzag machine stitch. For further texture interest, apply

◄ *Machine embroidery and rich beading on hand-printed fabric combine to lift a simply cut evening dress into the haute couture class.*

shapes of silver or gold kid. Beads can also be combined with smocking designs which look marvelous for evening or bridal dresses. For a peasant look, combine hand embroidery with wood and china or chalk beads. Padded appliqué and quilting also take on a new richness when combined with beading.

Printed fabric and beading

Printed fabrics can provide inspiration for the basis of a beaded embroidery design. On the elegant evening dress shown in this chapter, for instance, the beading is worked over a hand-printed design combined with free-motion embroidery. When working on printed fabrics, choose bold prints and select focal areas of the pattern to highlight. Small, complicated prints should be avoided as the beading will only complicate the design. Avoid over-beading a pattern or the result will be a confused mess. If you are not sure whether you have done enough, hang the beaded section somewhere where it can be viewed easily and leave it for a day or so. When you return to it, you will find it easier to be critical and be able to decide whether to add more beads or to leave it as it is.

Transferring designs

Method 1. Pricking and pouncing. Draw the design onto tracing paper and lay the paper face downward over a soft pad, such as a folded blanket or a sheet of felt. Perforate the lines of the design with a pin (or a sewing machine needle may be easier to handle), keeping the holes closely spaced. Baste the pricked design rough side uppermost (the right side up) to the fabric and, using a small round pad made from a piece of tightly rolled-up felt 2 inches square, dab powdered chalk through the holes. Use powdered chalk on dark colors and powdered charcoal mixed with a little chalk on light colors. This method is especially suitable for complex designs and designs which need to be repeated two or more times. Fix the pounced design by painting over the dotted lines with watercolor paint, using a very fine brush. Because the design is thus permanently marked onto the fabric, the lines of the design must be strictly followed during beading.

Method 2. Tracing. For beading on semi-transparent fabrics, place the design under the fabric and very carefully trace through using a hard lead pencil with a very fine point. Alternatively, trace the design onto tracing paper using a felt-tipped pen. Pin the design securely in position underneath the fabric, and with small running stitches follow the line of the design without working through the paper.

Method 3. Basting. Place the traced design onto the right side of the fabric and baste the outlines, using small stitches, through to the fabric. To remove the paper without damaging the fabric perforate it with a needle between and under each stitch, then tear the paper away carefully.

Calculating quantities

If the area to be beaded is large or includes a number of repeats, it is essential to work a sample of any design first to calculate how many beads are required.

Measure the length and depth of the worked sample and then work out how many repeats of the sample are required to cover the area to be beaded. Count the number of beads used on the sample and multiply this by the number of repeats required to find the total number of beads of each kind required.

Stretching beadwork

When planning a design, bear in mind the weight of the beads and their "pull" on the fabric. If the beading is likely to be heavy, use the fabric double, particularly when working with sheer fabrics, or for added strength mount each piece of the garment on unbleached muslin before beading.

Sometimes, a completed piece of beading may show signs of puckering, and if this happens the work will require stretching. Place two or three sheets of damp blotting paper over a wooden surface larger than the area of the finished work, such as a drawing board. Place the beading right side uppermost over the paper and, making sure that at least one edge of the work is straight, pin it out with gold-headed thumbtacks (which do not rust so easily) at about 2 inch intervals. Work around the embroidery, easing it into shape as you pin. Continue pinning until the pins are touching each other. Leave the work to dry for at least 24 hours.

If sequins have been used in the embroidery, extra care is needed. Some sequins are made on a basis of gelatine and curl up and melt when they come into contact with water. To prevent this, dampen the first sheet of paper only, and place a layer of dry paper over it before pinning out the work.

Ways with beads

Piling beads. Beads and sequins can be sewn piled on top of each other, and it is great fun to experiment with combinations of different shapes and surface qualities. For example, pile six sequins decreasing in size, some cup shaped, some flat and of different colors, topped with a small chalk bead to secure. The examples given in this chapter show eight permutations on the "round shape". Several beads sewn on at a time can give a lovely raised, loopy effect, two bugles sewn on at a time result in a spiky texture.

▲ *Top row: swing motifs for exotic fringes. Center and bottom row: eight variations of piling beads and sequins for encrusted designs*

Swing motifs. Sewing swing motifs can be fun, too, and these can be extended to fringes which can be as light and fragile or as heavy and chunky as desired. Some examples are shown in this chapter but the permutations are unlimited. Any of the swing motifs shown can be continued along the edge of fabric to make a fringe. For picot edgings, sew beads along the edge of the fabric, securing each bead with a tiny chalk bead. Different effects can be achieved depending on the shapes of the beads used.

Collector's Piece

Story in silk

This 17th century English silk embroidery illustrates the Old Testament story of Esther, the beautiful Jewish queen of Ahasuerus. The panel shows that after Ahasuerus has been pursuaded by Haman, his chief adviser, to exterminate the Jews, the Queen invites the King and Haman to a banquet, at which she names Haman as the persecutor of her people (left of panel).
The King orders Haman to be hanged (top left), and Mordecai, the Queen's uncle, rides in triumph, having been acknowledged for saving the King's life from assassins (top right).
As the King holds out his golden scepter to Esther, she asks for the revocation of the edict ordering the massacre of the Jews (center of panel).
The embroidered pictures of the 17th century were worked on linen canvas in petit point, and it is interesting to note that the stitches run from left to right on the right half of the panel, and from right to left on the left half.
Although this is probably because two embroiderers worked facing each other, an alternative theory suggests that the panel might have been worked this way to minimize the pull of tent stitch, which can sometimes result in distortion of a panel.
Pictures such as this were often a collection of anachronisms; the biblical characters are dressed in Stuart fashions, the court scenes are set in pastoral surroundings, and insects, flowers and animals, invariably out of scale to each other, abound.

Two friends to make

Dapple Pony and Dozy Dog are both filled with man-made wadding and so are fully washable. A graph for the pattern pieces is given on the opposite page.

Dapple Pony

You will need
For the pony:
- [ ] 1yd 36in wide cotton fabric
- [ ] ½oz thick uncut rug yarn or knitting yarn (for the mane and tail)
- [ ] Two 1¼in diameter buttons (for the eyes)
- [ ] 1½ to 2yd 36in Dacron wadding

- [ ] Strip of cardboard, 3in wide and 10in long
- [ ] Matching sewing thread, basting thread
- [ ] Pins

For pattern making:
- [ ] A sheet at least 20in square of 1in squared paper. Either rule brown paper or use graph paper
- [ ] Pencil
- [ ] Scissors

Making the pattern
Copy all the pattern pieces and their markings from the graph onto the squared paper. One square on the graph is equal to one 1 inch square on the paper.

The body piece is the entire outline of the pony, and the leg facing is the lower half of the pattern below line A to B. Cut out all the pattern pieces around their edges. Seam allowance is included on the pattern for all outer edges, but not on the edge A to B on the leg facings. On this edge ½ inch seam allowance must be added.

Cutting the fabric
Fold the cotton fabric in half and pin the pattern pieces to the double fabric.
Cut out 2 body pieces and 2 leg facing pieces.
Unpin the pattern pieces.

Making the pony
The mane. Wind the yarn around the 3 inch width of the cardboard until the entire length is covered. Machine stitch the loops of yarn together along one side by gradually withdrawing the cardboard as the yarn is stitched (figure 1).
The tail. Cut 3 strands of yarn each 15 inches long, tie them together at one end and braid 10 inches. Bind the braid, leaving 5 inches of yarn free at the end.

The body. Place the two body pieces together, right sides facing, and pin in the mane and tail where indicated on the graph. The greater part of the mane and tail lie inside the body at this stage and the beginning of the braided tail and line of stitches on the mane match the seam allowance edges of the body pieces.
Pin, baste and stitch all around the upper part of the body from A to B, enclosing the mane and tail in the process.
The leg facings. Place the leg facings together, right sides facing, and stitch them together along line A to B, leaving a 5 inch opening in the middle of the seam through which to insert the stuffing.
Place the joined leg facings between the joined body pieces, right sides together and edges matching. Pin, baste and stitch all seams, making sure that the leg facings join the body pieces firmly at A and B.
Snip into the seam allowance on all curves and turn the body right side out through the 5 inch opening.
Stuff the body and legs with the wadding, tearing the wadding into small pieces before inserting it. Stuff the legs very firmly. Close the opening with slip stitch.
Sew the eyes into position where marked on the graph.

Dozy Dog

You will need
- [ ] 1yd 36in wide cotton fabric
- [ ] Small scraps of felt in a pale color and black (for the eyes and nose)
- [ ] Wadding as for the pony
- [ ] Matching sewing thread, basting thread
- [ ] Pins
- [ ] Tracing paper
- [ ] Pattern making materials as for the pony

Make and cut out the pattern pieces for Dozy Dog as for the pony, adding ½ inch seam allowance to the line C to D on the leg facings.

Cutting the fabric
Fold the fabric in half, right

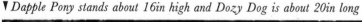

Dapple Pony stands about 16in high and Dozy Dog is about 20in long

sides facing, and pin the pattern pieces to the double fabric. Cut out 2 body pieces (the entire outline), 2 leg facings (the lower half of the dog below line C to D), 4 ear pieces, 2 tail pieces and a head gusset. Unpin the pattern pieces.

Making the dog
The tail. Place the tail pieces together, right sides facing, and stitch them together leaving the short, straight side open. Snip into the seam allowances on the curves and turn the tail right side out. Stuff with a little wadding and baste the opening together.

The body. Place the main body pieces together, right sides facing, and pin the tail between them where shown on the graph. Also, pin the head gusset into place with the front point of the head gusset matching point C. Baste and stitch all seams above C to D, stitching the tail and head gusset into place.

The leg facings. Join the leg facings as for the pony and stitch them into place. Snip into the seam allowance on all curves, and turn the dog right side out. Insert the stuffing through the opening left in the leg facings. Close the opening with slip stitch.

The eyes and nose. Tracing patterns for these features are given in figure **2**. Cut 2 outer eyes from pale colored felt and 2 inner eyes from black felt. Cut 1 nose from black felt. Sew the inner eyes to the outer eyes and sew the completed eyes onto the head where shown on the graph, using very small, neat stitches. Sew the nose onto the head where marked.

The ears. Join the ear pieces together in pairs, right sides facing, leaving an opening on the short, straight edge. Snip into the seam allowances on the curves and turn the ears right side out. Turn in the seam allowance on the openings and close with slip stitch. Press the ears carefully and hand sew them to the head where marked on the graph.

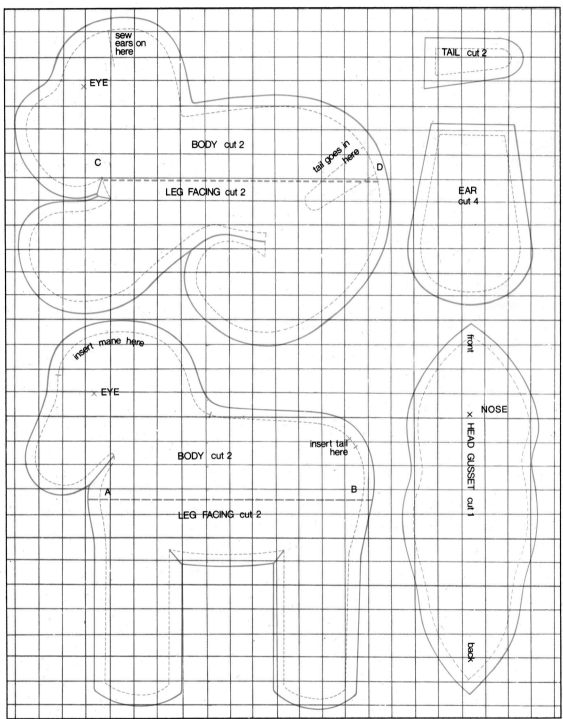

▲ *Graph for all the pattern pieces. Scale: 1 square = 1 inch. Pony = blue outline, dog = pink outline*

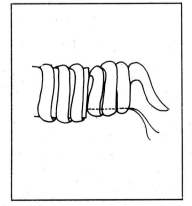

▼ **1.** *Stitching the mane*

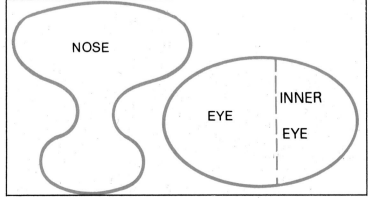

▼ **2.** *Dozy Dog: tracing patterns for the features*

Turning corners

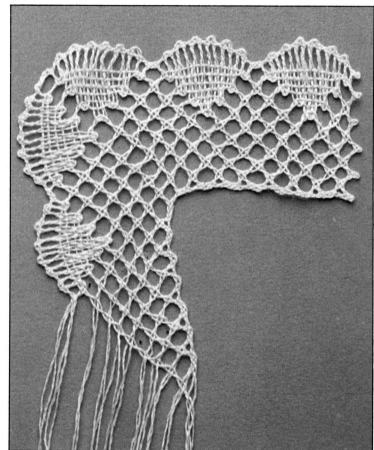

Because lace is frequently used as an edging, the technique of turning a corner is particularly important and useful. It is a surprisingly simple procedure, based on working down to a diagonal, then turning the work and continuing down from the diagonal. The straight edges can be worked to any length and in this way an edging can be made to fit a square or oblong piece of fabric.

Once this has been learned, and combined with the basic principles given in previous Bobbin Lace chapters, it will be possible to work, as most lace experts do, directly from photographs or actual samples. Detailed instructions will no longer be necessary and experience will come from copying as many different designs as possible.

A new stitch given in this chapter, called a spider, is frequently seen in samples of bobbin lace.

To work a corner
Place two bobbins at each starting point. A neater finish results from winding each pair onto the opposite ends of the same thread, thus starting off with a small loop rather than a knot.

This simple edging combines weave foundation stitch (see Bobbin lace chapter 2, page 514) with mesh stitch with one twist (see Bobbin lace chapter 3, page 590). The pricking is shown in two colors for greater clarity. First work all the holes which are marked in blue, then at point A, with two pairs of bobbins, work several half stitches one after the other to form a braid across to point B. Turn the work and continue down the pattern marked in red, starting with an ordinary stitch at B and picking up one pair of bobbins from the blue half at each adjoining pin hole.

Spider edging lace

This attractive piece of lace consists mainly of "spiders", a pattern frequently used in bobbin lace. The edging can be worked as a straight piece or can be taken around a corner as shown on the graph. This pattern requires fifty pairs of bobbins.

To make a spider
Twist all pairs three times and start with a whole stitch at point 1. Continue until 9 is reached and then place a pin in the center hole. With the two center pairs, work point 10 and continue until 18 is reached. Twist all pairs three times.

If the spider has more legs they are worked in the same way. The only difference will be a fatter body.

Marking out the spider edging
Place a dot in the corner of every other square and build the pattern out as shown. The size of the edging will depend on the scale of the graph paper.

▲ *Sample of a lace edging corner which is charted below*
▼ *Two-color pricking for turning the corner*

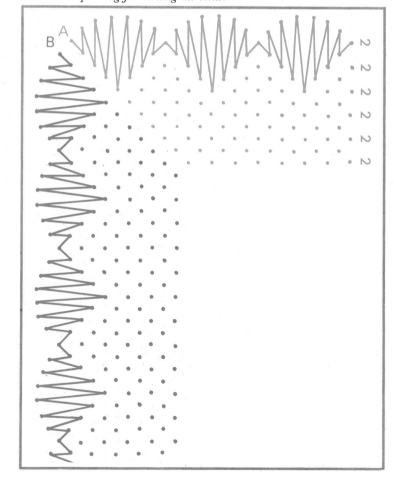

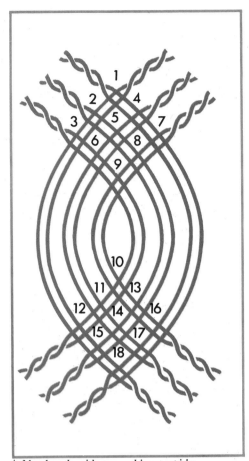

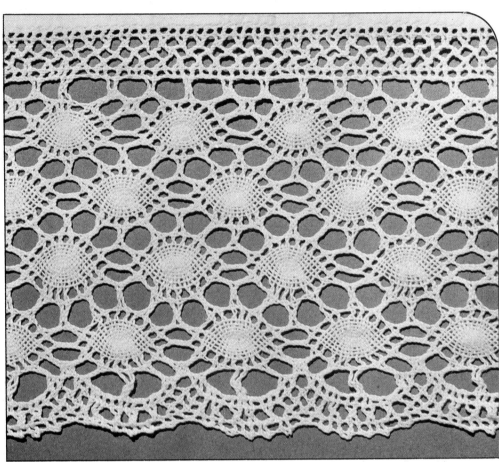

▲ Numbered guide to working a spider　　▲ Close-up detail of the spider edging lace

▼ Graph for working a corner section of the spider edging lace, a straight section of which is shown above

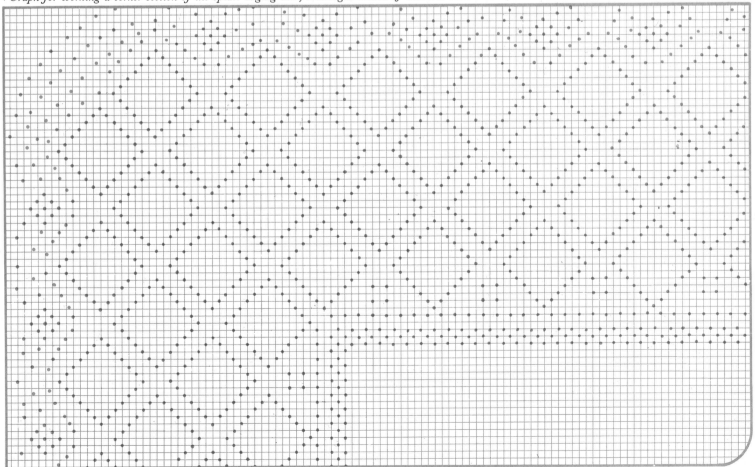

Working with lace fabrics

Lace comes in so many different forms that here it would be impossible to describe every type in one chapter. Many countries have their own traditional laces, handmade by craftsmen over many generations, which are of a perfection no machine could ever achieve. But machines have taken over and today many manufacturers are producing laces of great variety and of a high standard and quality.

This chapter concentrates on the main types of machine-made dress laces you are likely to find in your local stores, and sets out to give you general advice on how to handle these delicate fabrics. There are useful tips on buying lace for garment making, and choosing the right style to make the most of the design of the fabric.

Making lace garments requires patience and a knowledge of the fabric in order to work with it in the correct way. For instance, many laces can only be worked by hand, and at the end of this chapter you will find some techniques that will help you to begin to acquire this particular skill.

The beautiful wedding dress on page 1319 is a Vogue Pattern and shows lace in its most romantic mood.

Types of lace

The difference in the construction of various machine-made laces divides them into three main groups.

Group 1. Knitted and crocheted lace.
Group 2. Woven lace.
Group 3. Embroidered lace.

Under these main groups you will find lace both for garment making and for trimming.

Group 1. Knitted and crocheted lace

Under this heading comes raschel knitted lace (figure 1), which is the cheapest form of lace on the market today. It is cheap because the construction is simple and therefore fast.

This category includes crochet-type lace which comes in the form of curtain lace (figure 2). Curtain lace, as its name suggests, is, strictly speaking, a home furnishing lace, but manufacturers are selling more and more today for dress wear in keeping with current fashion demand.

Group 2. Woven lace

Woven, or Leavers lace (figure 3), is perhaps the most popular form of lace available today and is easy to obtain through most retail outlets. Here, the threads are twisted, rather than knitted

1. Raschel knitted lace showing the edge finish for all-over lace; 2. Crochet-type curtain lace; 3. Woven, or Leavers, lace showing a flouncing edge finish; 4. Re-embroidered ribbon lace; 5. Guipure lace▶

1

2

3

4

5

together. The background of woven lace is usually net, which may be of even design or may form part of the intricate design of the lace itself.

A variety of designs are to be found in this category. Because weaving is so versatile manufacturers can achieve a greater variation in design than with any other form of lace construction.

Group 3. Embroidered lace

Embroidered lace ranges from eyelet embroidery on woven fabric to raschel or Leavers lace, which is re-embroidered with ribbon (figure **4**) or braid or cord over the original design to give a more bulky or textured appearance. Some re-embroidered laces have very heavy braid incorporated into the design, and this is done either in the process of manufacture, or the braid is applied afterwards.

Guipure lace (figure **5**) is a special type of embroidered lace and may be placed under this heading, although this is the only lace not made on a lace machine. It is made on a Schiffli embroidery machine which originated in Germany. Here the lace is embroidered onto an acetate fabric which is dissolved in a special acid solution after the embroidery has been completed.

In spite of the open-work appearance of guipure lace, it is a heavy, chunky type of lace and falls in the more expensive price bracket.

Edge finishes

When you buy lace you will find that there is a choice of two edge finishes, and this may determine the yardage available to you.

All-over lace (see figure **1**). Here the design is extended from side to side and all-over lace is usually available in any yardage desired.

Flouncing (see figure **3**). This lace has one or both edges of the fabric length finished with scallops. In most cases flouncing is only obtainable in lengths of 4½ to 5 yards, although many stores are willing to cut you a shorter length if desired. The only variation is raschel flouncing which is available in any yardage.

Lace widths

Raschel lace. This is usually available in 46 to 47 inch widths, both all-over lace and flouncing.

Crochet-type curtain lace. This usually comes in 43 to 44 inch widths.

Leavers lace. The all-over lace is usually in 34 to 46 inch widths. Flouncing varies from 34 to 36 inch, 47 to 48 inch and 70 to 72 inch widths, the latter being available in white only for bridal wear, usually with flouncing on both edges.

Guipure lace. Here the widths are usually 36 to 48 inches.

Occasionally you might find both guipure and raschel laces in 54 inch widths, but these types are usually imported from Germany or Austria.

Fiber content

Raschel and Leavers laces are usually composed of a nylon and rayon mixture. Exceptions may be found in a raschel all nylon lace and Leavers nylon and cotton, or all cotton, laces.

Curtain laces are all cotton, as, on the whole, are guipures.

Taking care of lace

Although the fiber content of a lace may suggest that it can be washed, manufacturers recommend dry cleaning only because of the finishing processes involved which, with washing, can result in shrinkage and design distortion.

The only exception is an all nylon lace which can be washed with comparative safety, but even here be sure to check on the washability at the time of purchase. Also, you must take into consideration the lining fabric being used.

But, as a general rule, it is best not to risk washing lace because there are too many intervening factors.

▲ **6.** and **7.** Left: simple evening dress in curtain lace. Butterick pattern; Right: tunic top in guipure lace, plain pants. Vogue pattern

Buying lace and choosing the style

Many dressmakers cherish the ambition to make a lace dress, and perhaps the most obvious opportunity arrives with a wedding or a special dinner or cocktail engagement. Wearing lace has long been associated with special occasions, but today there are many types of laces which are suitable for more casual styling, such as tunic pants suits and simple summer day and evening dresses. The Vogue and Butterick patterns in figures **6** and **7** are ideal styles.

It is therefore important when buying lace that you not only have an idea of the style of garment you wish to make but also the occasion for which it is to be worn.

If this is your very first attempt at dressmaking with lace, it is advisable to choose a raschel all-over lace where you are less likely to run into trouble with widths and yardage and construction of the garment itself.

Some lace designs require careful matching, so look at the design carefully when buying and, if there is a very large pattern repeat, make sure that you buy sufficient yardage.

How to use lace

○ All-over lace can usually be cut like any ordinary fabric with a surface design.

○ Flouncing, by its very nature, dictates the design of the garment. This type of lace is put to best use when the flouncing becomes part of the design. An illustration of this is given in figure **8** using a Butterick pattern.

8. Butterick Pattern showing flouncing used on the neckline as part of the design

If you decide not to use the flouncing and cut it off, remember that the fabric width will be decreased quite considerably. It would also rob you of a lovely ready-made edge and design interest.

Lace very rarely has a direction for the grain line or fall woven in, and it can be turned when cutting to enable you to make the most of the finished edge. With flouncing you can therefore have the scallops in almost any place you wish.

On large areas, such as skirts, you can
1318

use the scallops around the hem if the skirt is cut straight. But skirts cut with flare would make the scalloped hemline uneven.

If you want to use the scallops on a rounded shape it is necessary to cut the scallops carefully away from the edge of the fabric and then appliqué them by hand. This delicate process is explained later in the chapter under hand-sewing techniques.

○ All lightweight laces should, whenever possible, be used as a single layer of fabric and not mounted. Mounting destroys the fine, see-through appearance and the full effect of the delicate fabric will be lost.

○ Heavy laces should not be used lavishly to create folds and drapes—simple designs are best. Too lavish use of a heavy lace will obliterate the design of the fabric. To reveal the design, mount the lace on a matching or contrasting fabric; this also helps to support the weight of the lace and avoids dragging. Garments made from a combination of mounting fabric and lace tend to be heavy, and the tailored or sculptured styles are the best.

Garments which are cut in small sections are ideal for heavy lace because there is plenty of anchorage in the seams.

Mounting and lining fabrics
For both mounting or lining lace fabrics choose a smooth surfaced fabric such as rayon taffeta, slipper satin or pure silk taffeta.

Sewing lace
Since there are many types of laces, there are also many ways in which to sew them. The method chosen often depends upon the type of garment it is made into and the kind of wear it will receive.

On some laces, hand-sewing is the only method possible, and this is covered later in the chapter. The methods below apply to machine stitching.

Seams. With many ordinary dress laces the seams can be stitched by machine, but heavy lace is rarely stitched on a machine. When stitching seams in unmounted lace, trim the seam allowances after stitching to not more than $\frac{1}{4}$ inch and whip stitch the raw edges together.

A machine zigzag finish on raw edges should be confined to the stronger nylon laces. Soft laces gather up under this treatment as the seam itself stretches, and although this can usually be pressed back into shape, the seam will distort again during hanging and wear.

Threads and stitches. If you are using fine or open-work lace, which may have large areas of net between the design, use fine sewing thread in the machine.

Uneven tension of the stitches can have

a gathering effect on the lace and the seams will break, so first try the stitch tension on layers of lace scraps.

Also test the stitch length to find the most suitable for the lace you are using. The stitches should be small and neat but remember, if you have to rip the seams, stitches which are too small will only break the delicate fabric.

Edges and hems. On edges requiring facing, to avoid thickness and the confusion of double color and pattern use fine matching net and work this in the same way as a bias facing.

Hems in all-over lace can be turned up in the usual way. There is too much movement in a hem for a net finish.

What to wear under a lace dress
The fitted slip in Dressmaking chapter 55, p. 1096 gives a bare shouldered look and is an ideal garment to wear under lace.

If you don't want a separate undergarment, make the opening of the slip correspond with the opening of the lace dress and catch slip and dress together. A waisted style, too, can be attached to the waistline of the slip.

Mounting and lining lace
For lace garments without waist seams, the garment and the lining are made separately and then stitched together at the neckline and armholes only.

If the dress is waisted, make the bodice and skirt lining separately and stitch them into the waist seam of the dress as well as the neckline and armholes.

Sleeves are mostly left unlined, unless they are long and fitted, in which case the strain is supported by an underlining of matching net.

When mounting heavy lace make sure that the lace does not tighten and form pockets of surplus fabric in the mounting. This could be the result of undetectable stretch in the lace or shrinkage, through heat, of the lace when pressing. So, to minimize the latter, always press the lace first and mount it with care.

When pressing, avoid stretching the lace by moving the iron over it in a lifting and pressing motion and make sure that the lace is supported over the sides of the ironing board to prevent drag.

Openings
Never insert a zipper into lace unless it is mounted. Instead, make a separate placket-type fastening as shown in figure **9**, which is held together with tiny hooks and metal bars. Buttonhole stitch over the bars and hooks with matching thread so that they will not show. This type of fastening can be used with most laces.

If the fastening is not subject to any strain, it may come undone. To prevent this, alternate the hooks and bars with tiny snap fasteners.

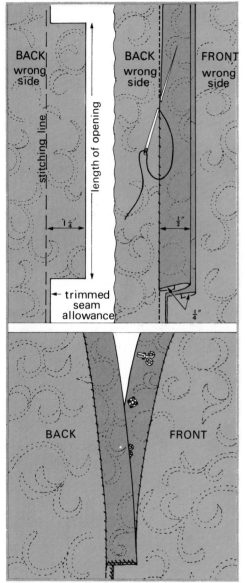

▲ 9. *Steps in making a placket-type fastening*

Fitting a lace dress

Never fit lace too closely at the underarm, waist or hips because it wouldn't stand the strain. It is therefore especially important when fitting to try all those movements which are going to put strain on the seams.

With some laces, you may find that the ease in the seams of the pattern cannot be dealt with as in other fabrics, and "bounces". If this happens, fit these areas very carefully by taking out the ease as far as movement will allow.

You may have to leave the hem of the dress until the very last stages of sewing since gathers and weight can affect the evenness of the hemline.

Vogue Pattern made in Leavers lace   ►

▲ **10.** *Appliquéd scallops: cutting the scallops away from the edge of the lace*

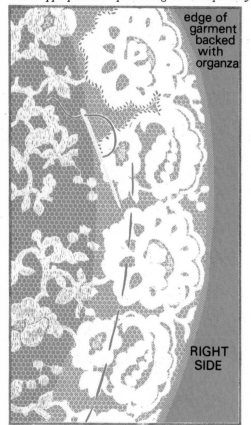

edge of garment backed with organza

RIGHT SIDE

▲ **11.** *Working the scallops onto the shaped edge*

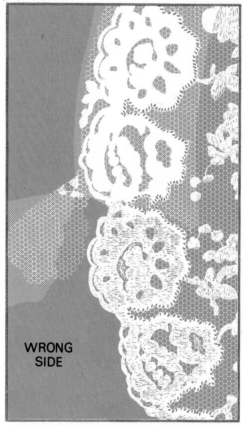

WRONG SIDE

▲ **12.** *Trimming the finished scalloped edge*

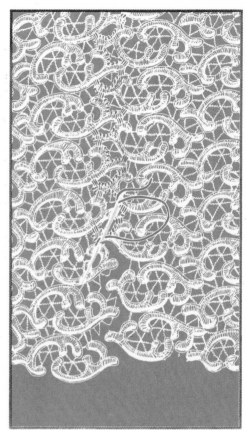

▲ **13.** *Joining the motifs on guipure lace*

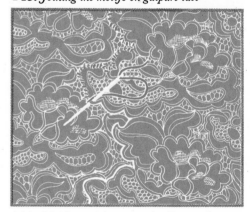

▲ **14.** *Making a join on heavier Leavers lace*

Hand-sewing techniques

Of the numerous hand-sewing techniques which are applied to lace, two of the most useful are given here—how to appliqué flouncing scallops to a rounded edge, and how to join lace for a hand-sewn seam.

Appliquéd scallops

If you want to use scallops on a rounded shape, such as a neckline, flared skirt or sleeve hem, first make sure that the design of the lace can be worked in this way.

Flouncing varies so much that sometimes the scallops form just a simple edging to the lace design, and sometimes the design extends deep into the lace before a

1320

borderline for cutting is reached.

So, having satisfied yourself that the lace is suitable, carefully cut the scallops away from the lace fabric (figure **10**).

Then cut the dress as you want and appliqué the lace scallops to the shaped edge after the dress has been assembled. Use a silk thread and work the appliqué over a piece of fine, pure silk organza to avoid distorting the pattern (figure **11**).

Carefully trim away the organza and lace after the appliqué is finished (figure **12**). If the scalloped edges are somewhat untidy and weak, secure them with a row of whip stitching, again using silk thread.

This will create a fine cord-like effect. You will find that a detailed, illustrated reference to whip stitching is given in Dressmaking 52, p. 1036, figures 7 and 8.

Joining lace

Seams on some laces have to be avoided completely and any necessary joins worked by hand following the design of the lace. Use a suitable hand-sewing thread for the lace and work the join in an overcasting motion.

On guipure lace the edges of the lace design are drawn together to form the join in the continuous repeat of the design (figure **13**).

On heavier Leavers lace the outline of the lace is lapped and matched so that the top side of the join provides the final outline (figure **14**).

Joining lace by hand is delicate work and the join must be so fine that it cannot be detected from a reasonable distance. The final effect, however, is worthwhile.